Demographic Projection Techniques for Regions and Smaller Areas

H. Craig Davis

Demographic Projection Techniques for Regions and Smaller Areas: A Primer

UBCPress / Vancouver

Printed in Canada on acid-free paper ∞

ISBN 0-7748-0501-3

Canadian Cataloguing in Publication Data

Davis, H. Craig
    Demographic projection techniques for regions and smaller areas

    Includes bibliographical references and index.
    ISBN 0-7748-0501-3

    1. Population forecasting–Methodology. 2. Demography–Methodology. I. Title.

HB849.53.D38 1994   304.6'01'12   C94-910879-0

UBC Press gratefully acknowledges the ongoing support to its publishing program from the Canada Council, the Province of British Columbia Cultural Services Branch, and the Department of Communications of the Government of Canada.

UBC Press
University of British Columbia
6344 Memorial Road
Vancouver, BC V6T 1Z2
(604) 822-3259
Fax: (604) 822-6083

To the memory of my father,
Harrell Ross Davis

Contents

Preface

This primer is intended to be an introductory guide to undertaking projections of an area's population and the elements of population change: fertility, mortality, and migration. For the purposes of this text, an area may range in size from a city block to a municipality, county, or metropolitan region, but is generally considered to be smaller than a province or a state. Four basic approaches to constructing projections are considered in the text: mathematical extrapolation, comparative methods, the cohort-survival model, and models that focus on migration.

As it is assumed that the reader has little background in demography, mathematics, or statistics, the text focuses on presenting fundamental material in a nontechnical manner. A list of selected readings is presented at the end of the book for each chapter for those who wish to pursue the chapter's content further. These readings have been specifically chosen for students and practitioners with limited mathematical backgrounds. More advanced readings are cited in the chapter notes at the end of the book.

Chapter 1 contains a general discussion of the value and purpose of population projections and distinguishes projections from forecasts and estimates. Mathematical extrapolation is the subject of Chapters 2 and 3. Five mathematical functions that are commonly used in making projections are considered in turn: the linear, exponential, polynomial, hyperbolic, and modified exponential functions. Each is treated in the same manner: its properties are described, its transformation into a linear form is shown, and a numerical illustration of its use in projection is given.

At the end of Chapter 3, a four-step procedure for choosing among the five functions and making a projection based on linear regression is presented. (Cursory reviews of the relevant elements of linear regression analysis and of simple applications of logarithms are offered in Appendices 1 and 2, respectively.) For the purposes of practical applications, it is useful for the reader to be familiar with the basic operations of a computer spreadsheet such as Lotus 1-2-3, Excel, or Quattro Pro.

Chapter 4 is concerned with the comparative methods approach to making projections. Such projections are made by comparing observations of the population size in the area of interest with that of another area, generally a larger one. The focus of Chapter 5 is the projection of population with the cohort-survival model, using population groups of uniform age and sex. Numerical illustrations of commonly used measures of fertility and mortality are included in this chapter. Discussion in Chapter 6 centres on what is generally the most volatile of the demographic elements: migration. Basic concepts and the underlying determinants of migration are discussed, and procedures for estimating past migration and projecting future migration are reviewed.

For their assistance in making the exposition of the text material more clear and concise, I wish to thank Professor Henry Hightower and the many students who made helpful comments on earlier drafts of the text. In particular, I wish to thank my colleague David Baxter for his thoughtful and invaluable suggestions. Any remaining errors in the texts or sins of omission are, of course, entirely my responsibility.

Demographic Projection Techniques for Regions and Small Areas

Chapter 1

Introduction

The Value of Population Projections

Demographic information—data regarding the number and characteristics of people in an area at one or more points in time—is of critical importance to many activities in both the public and private sectors of society. For example, it bears directly on the operations of commercial enterprises in two basic ways. First, for many businesses, particularly those in retail trade and service activities, the sales volume in the local market is highly correlated with the level of population. Changes in sales can be expected to vary directly with changes in the number of consumers. Depending on the product, sales can also be sensitive to changes in the age and sex composition of the local population. Further, for some goods and services (e.g., clothing, foodstuffs, broadcasting, advertising), ethnicity and cultural aspects of the populace may be critical.[1]

Second, demographic information can be important to firms in regard to their labour force. If a firm is considering expanding or moving from the area from which it draws its present labour force, it must be assured that it can attract a sufficient number of workers from the local population.[2] Generally, the larger the firm, the more important this consideration. For firms that draw their workforce from specific segments of the population, the age and sex composition of the population may also be significant.

Demographic information is vital to the public sector as well. Governments use population figures to express a range of statistics (from gross domestic product and school enrolments to violent crimes and traffic fatalities) on a per capita basis. This is done to facilitate comparisons between geographic regions and for a single region over time. Demographic information is also critical to public-sector planning. For example, in the delivery of public services, underestimates of future population levels may readily result in crowded public facilities and subsequent costly crash programs for expansion, while overestimates may lead to excess capacity and overstaffing and thus to a misallocation of resources.[3]

Whether for planning in the private sector (e.g., for the expansion or relocation of commercial facilities) or in the public sector (e.g., for the provision of day-care centers, schools, libraries, recreational facilities, parks, hospital beds, utilities, and protective services), demographic information, particularly projections of future populations and their characteristics, is vital to efficient decision-making.[4]

Isserman and Fisher[5] expand the discussion of the usefulness of demographic projections by considering them as inputs to the planning process that, in turn, can be utilized to alter the projected future. Adopting a proactive stance, the authors consider three beneficial ways in which population projections can be utilized by planners. First, a projection of an undesirable future can serve as a "resounding call to arms" for a community to mobilize itself to alter the underlying conditions. For example, if it is projected that the community's youth will be out-migrating in significant numbers because of the lack of employment opportunities, planners can attempt to undertake initiatives resulting in the provision of such opportunities. In this context the projection is taken not as a state that the community should prepare to meet in the most efficient manner possible, but as a future whose desirability is to be considered. The projection serves primarily as a stimulant to this consideration.[6]

Second, a range of projections revealing a significant variance in future population levels may serve to alert a community to the degree of uncertainty associated with its future and to generate actions to reduce this uncertainty. For example, projections for a community whose economic fortunes are dependent on world prices of a particular mineral may range from boom times to bust. Such projections may result in an intensified effort by a community to gain a greater measure of control over its economic and demographic prospects in order to reduce potential uncertainty. Somewhat paradoxically, the success of the planning process in this context will be measured at least partially by the resulting *divergence* between the projected and actual outcomes.

Third, closely related to the above, projections may be used as teaching devices in the consideration of different futures. Assumptions underlying each of the projections become part of the discussion for responding to various options. In addition to generating, say, possible futures X, Y, and Z, projection models may be run backwards to determine what conditions would have to be met to result in X, Y, or Z. Moen[7] argues for just such an approach, stating that

> the best way a community, region, and state can predict and plan
> for population growth and change is through active projections and
> planning—deciding what would be desirable and then designing poli-
> cies and programs to achieve that future. Population projection mod-

els would then be used more as a research tool, e.g., to determine patterns of labor force participation and growth rates that would lead to a desired population growth rate and size...methods would not change radically; instead, the model would simply be run backwards. Data that formerly drove such models would become results. What were formerly results would drive the model.

In each of these three beneficial ways in which projections can affect the planning process, future conditions are assumed to be alterable by present community actions. The future is shaped not only by external forces but by the planning process itself.

Projections, Forecasts, and Estimates: Definitions

The terms "projection" and "forecast" are frequently used interchangeably in practice as well as in the demographic literature. In this text we shall follow the advice of a number of authors who have argued for drawing a distinction between these terms.[8] A projection is a *conditional* statement, an "if...then" declaration. It is the numerical outcome of an accepted set of assumptions. For example, the statement "if the population growth trend over the last ten years continues, the population of Smallville five years from now will be 5,175" is a projection. In contrast, a forecast is an *unconditional* statement; it is what the analyst concludes to be the most likely outcome. The pronouncement that "Smallville's population five years hence will be 5,175" is a forecast. It is a prediction that at a future date, the population will be 5,175. (Throughout the text the terms "forecast" and "prediction" are used interchangeably.) Unless the analyst makes a mathematical error, a projection is never "wrong," since it is merely the result of numerical calculations based on given conditions. Forecasts, however, can be proved right or wrong by events. To the extent that the population of Smallville five years in the future deviates from 5,175, the forecast is in error. The projection stands, however, since it merely states that a particular population size would have resulted had a specified assumption (a continuation of the growth trend of the past ten years) been met.

Because the accuracy of projections is independent of events, analysts can perhaps be forgiven a preference for producing projections rather than forecasts.[9] Users of projections, however, understandably treat them as forecasts, since their decisions must be based on expectations of future population levels. Population projections are thus frequently treated as population forecasts.

Although the two terms differ in definition, procedures for projections and forecasts are the same. In making a projection, the analyst constructs a set of assumptions and calculates a result. In making a forecast, the analyst follows a similar procedure but chooses that set of assumptions he or she believes to be the most likely.

> The same formal method may be used for both projecting and fore-casting. In each case, the main purpose of the method is to calculate the numerical consequences (the "then") of the underlying assump-tions (the "if"). The key difference is that the forecaster is willing to take responsibility for identifying the assumptions which are most likely to be true. Technique, data, and modeling skill are involved in getting from the assumption to the impacts, but judgment, wisdom, persistence, imagination, and luck are needed to make those assump-tions correctly. It is at the level of making assumptions, particularly assumptions of the likely future course of events, that the technical exercise of projection becomes the high art of forecasting.[10]

A forecast, then, can be thought of as the most likely projection. Although the focus of the text is on projections, it is to be realized that in many cases the projections will serve as forecasts.

The word "estimate," when used in reference to population levels or composi-tions, is generally reserved for current and past populations.

> An *estimate* is an indirect measure of a condition that *exists* or *has existed*, and which, in principle, could be or could have been measured directly. Estimates are therefore made because direct measurement data are not yet available or because it is (or was) impractical to collect such data.[11]

For example, the statement "the present population of Smallville is 4,825" con-stitutes an *estimate* of Smallville's population. Estimates are frequently made to provide the basis for constructing projections and forecasts. In non-census years, estimations of populations of municipalities and sub-municipal areas are commonly based on estimates of occupied housing.[12]

The Basic Demographic Equation

For practically all areas, the size of the population within the area continuously changes from one period to the next. In each case, this change is composed of four basic demographic processes: births, deaths, in-migration, and out-migration. The change in the total population of a particular locality over any period can thus be expressed in terms of a 'bookkeeping' equation as the net result of the four processes.

$$P_1 - P_0 = B - D + IM - OM \qquad (1.1)$$

where P_1, P_0 = the populations at times 1 and 0, respectively;
   B, D   = births and deaths during the period 0–1; and
   IM, OM = in- and out-migration during the period 0–1, respectively.

The net contribution to the change in population through births and deaths is termed "reproductive change" or "natural increase (decrease)." The net impact on the population stock resulting from in- and out-migration is termed "net migration." Whenever possible, a projection of population should be undertaken in terms of the component parts shown in equation (1.1). The distinction between natural increase (B - D) and net migration (IM - OM) should first be made so that the contributions of the two processes to the change in population are not confused. This distinction is frequently critical to the projection of future population levels. Depending on the circumstances under which the projection is made, it is often useful to disaggregate the change further into its four basic demographic components (B, D, IM, OM). Unfortunately, however, the division of population change into its component parts is not always possible, and the projection process must proceed at a higher level of aggregation.

Overview of the Book

This book discusses the principal approaches to making demographic projections: mathematical extrapolations, comparative methods, cohort-survival, and migration models. Chapters 2 and 3 of the text are concerned with mathematical extrapolation. Extrapolation is commonly used to project the size of a population and is also frequently employed in projecting other demographic variables (e.g., the ratio of local to parent population, birth rates, death rates, migration rates) in conjunction with one or more of the other three approaches. This particular projection technique thus receives the most attention.

In Chapter 3 a four-step projection procedure is outlined that is used throughout the remainder of the text. The projection of population size by comparing the growth pattern of the population under study with that of another population is the subject of Chapter 4. Chapter 5 is concerned with what is likely the most commonly employed technique of population projection: the cohort-survival model. In contrast to mathematical extrapolation techniques and comparative methods, which focus on the projection of population *size*, the cohort-survival model is used to project not only population size but population *composition* in terms of age and sex groupings (cohorts). Migration, generally the most volatile component of the basic demographic equation, must be projected independently of the primary cohort-survival model. The various determinants of migration and the basic techniques for estimating and projecting migration are the subjects of Chapter 6.

Chapter 2

Mathematical Extrapolation I

To extrapolate is to infer the unknown from the known. Under the assumption that population is a function of time, extrapolation involves projecting future population on the basis of observed magnitudes of the population in the past. One approach is simply to plot the magnitudes of past population on a graph of population vs. time, such as that shown below, and to extend the curve into the future by hand or by means of a graphic artist's aide such as a French curve (see Figure 1).

Alternatively, one may describe the pattern of past population growth by application of a mathematical function.[1] The function may be used to describe how the population changed over time in the past and to identify how the population might change over time in the future. While there exists a considerable number of mathematical functions from which to choose, in the next two chapters we shall consider five functions that are commonly employed in demography: linear, exponential, polynomial, hyperbolic, and modified exponential. Familiarity with the application of these five functions will readily enable the reader to employ any number of other mathematical functions for extrapolation purposes.

The linear function describes a population trend of relatively constant numeric change (positive or negative). It is commonly the most appropriate function to track the population growth of small, slow-growing communities. Estimates of the linear function's parameters can be obtained through simple linear regression analysis (see Appendix A).

The exponential function describes the path over time of a population undergoing a constant rate of change. It is appropriately applied, for example, to project the population of a community that is rapidly expanding with no significant constraint to the growth process perceived within the projection period. The parameters of the exponential function can be estimated by regression analysis, but only after the function has been transformed into an equivalent linear expression by means

8

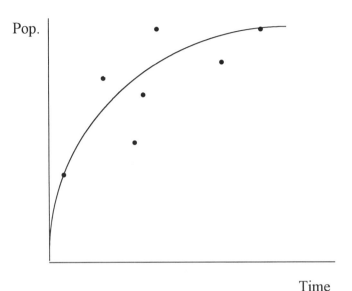

Figure 1. Population vs. time

of logarithms (see Appendix B).

A polynomial function is sometimes used in demographic analysis instead of the exponential function to better represent a population that is rapidly growing or declining. Compared with the exponential function, polynomial functions can conform to greater degrees of non-linearity.

Depending on the values of its parameters, the hyperbolic function approximates either the growth curve of the modified exponential function or the decay curve of the exponential function.

The last function to be considered—the modified exponential curve—is discussed in Chapter 3. This function differs from the first four in that it places an upper bound on growth (or a lower bound on decline).

For each of the five functions considered in this chapter and the next, the exposition includes the basic mathematical expression of the function, a graph of the function, and a numerical illustration of the use of the function to extrapolate the observed values of a hypothetical population. (A summary of the functions, including the principal steps in their applications to making projections, is presented in Chapter 3.) Although the focus of this chapter and the next is on the simple extrapolation of the magnitudes of total population, it is again important to note that the functions considered are also used, in practice, to generate values of various other demographic components (e.g., age– and sex–specific rates of births, deaths, and migration). These latter uses will be considered further in the chapters to follow.

The Linear Function

The simplest and most familiar of the functions[2] to be discussed in Chapters 2 and 3 is the straight line,

$$y = a + bx \tag{2.1}$$

Equation (2.1) tells us that y is a function of x. The values of y, the dependent variable, on the left-hand side of the equation, depend on values of x, the independent variable on the right-hand side. Further, equation (2.1) states that y varies linearly with x. That is, if one were to plot values of y associated with values of x, the result would be a straight line, as shown in Figure 2.

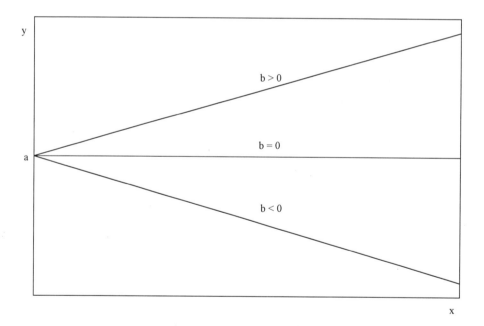

Figure 2. The linear function

From Figure 2, values of the independent variable x are read from the abscissa or x-axis; values of the dependent variable y are read from the ordinate or y-axis. The precise location on the graph of the line that the function of equation (2.1) traces depends on the values of the two parameters, or coefficients, a and b.

On the graph in Figure 2, a is the y-axis intercept, the value of y when x is zero: $y = a + (0)x = a$. The b coefficient determines the slope of the line. To see that this is indeed the case, let us focus on the first two pairs of observations: (x_1, y_1) and (x_2, y_2). From equation (2.1) we may write

$$y_1 = a + bx_1 \qquad (2.2)$$

$$y_2 = a + bx_2 \qquad (2.3)$$

Subtracting equation (2.2) from equation (2.3) yields

$$y_2 - y_1 = (a + bx_2) - (a + bx_1) = b(x_2 - x_1) \qquad (2.4)$$

Solving for b,

$$b = \frac{y_2 - y_1}{x_2 - x_1} = \frac{\Delta y}{\Delta x} = slope \qquad (2.5)$$

where the Greek letter "Δ" is the standard mathematical expression for the phrase "change in" and $\frac{\Delta y}{\Delta x}$ (the change in y resulting from a change in x) is by definition the slope of the line.[3]

For demographic projections, the constant slope, b, of the linear function implies a constant numerical change in the size of the population over time periods of equal length. The population change described by a linear function is thus a constant absolute amount over each period, past and future.

A Numerical Illustration

Suppose the following population data pertaining to population P_t at time t were recorded:

t:	0	1	2	3	4
P_t:	1,000	1,203	1,386	1,609	1,806
$P_t - P_{t-1}$:	–	203	183	223	197

From a casual inspection of the increments of population added each year ($P_t - P_{t-1}$) and the graph of the data in Figure 3 for times 0–4, it is decided to estimate a linear relationship between P_t and t as specified by equation (2.6).

$$P_t = a + bt \qquad (2.6)$$

Once the mathematical relationship between population and time, i.e., the trend of population over time, has been established, one may use it to project the population to $t = 5$ and beyond. The immediate task, then, is to estimate values of the coefficients a and b in equation (2.6).

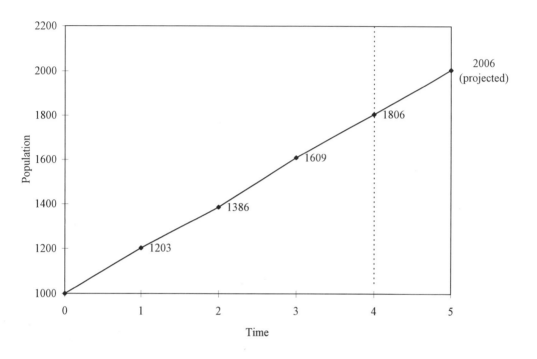

Figure 3. Linear population growth

Use of the linear regression capabilities of spreadsheet software to construct estimates $\hat{a}$ and $\hat{b}$ of a and b, respectively, will produce results such as those shown below. (A review of linear regression to construct estimates of coefficients in a linear equation and a general discussion of the regression output as shown here can be found in Appendix A.)

Regression Output:

Constant	997.2
Std Err of Y Est	9.770705
R Squared	0.999297
No. of Observations	5
Degrees of Freedom	3

X Coefficient(s)	201.8	
Std Error of Coeff.	3.089768	

Regression Equation: $P_t = 997.2 + 201.8t$

Given the above values of 997.2 for $\hat{a}$ and 201.8 for $\hat{b}$, our projected value for population at $t = 5$ is thus $P_5 = 997.2 + 201.8(5) = 2,006.$[4] The projected value is shown in Figure 3.

The Exponential Function

The exponential function is commonly used in demographic projections.[5] In its general form, it may be expressed as

$$y = ab^x \qquad (2.7)$$

where a and b are constants, the latter raised to the power of x. As can be seen from the graph of the function in Figure 4, the relationship between the two variables is non-linear.

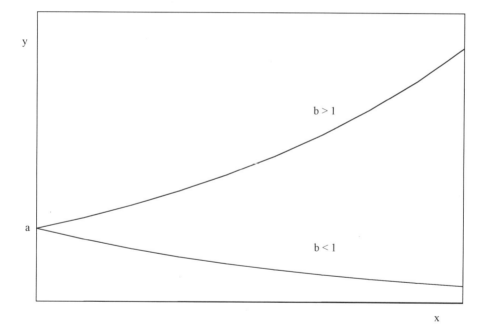

Figure 4. The exponential function

At x equal to 0, $b^0 = 1$ and y thus has a value of a, which is the "y-intercept." If the value of b exceeds one, y increases non-linearly without limit as x increases. The larger the value of b, the greater the rate of growth of y. With b equal to one, y is constant at a value of a. For all positive values of b less than one, y decreases toward zero. That is, as x increases, the value of y progressively decreases toward (but never quite reaches) zero. The variable y is said to approach zero "asymptotically." The smaller the value of b in this case, the more rapidly y approaches zero. The path traced by y when $0 < b < 1$ is referred to as one of "exponential decay."

In the previous section, it was seen that the linear function resulted in constant *numeric* change; in contrast, the exponential function results in a constant *rate* of change. To illustrate, suppose that we have n pairs of observations of x and y. We may write

$$y_1 = ab^{x_1} \tag{2.8}$$

$$y_2 = ab^{x_2} \tag{2.9}$$

$$\vdots$$

$$y_n = ab^{x_n} \tag{2.10}$$

The growth rate over any period is constant and equal to b, as can be seen from equation (2.11), which shows the growth rate between arbitrarily selected time t and the time of the previous observation $t - 1$.

$$\frac{y_t}{y_{t-1}} = \frac{ab^t}{ab^{t-1}} = b^{t-(t-1)} = b \tag{2.11}$$

The parameter b is raised to a power equal to the difference between t and $t - 1$, or simply one. The exponential is thus the function of a constant rate of growth or decay, depending on whether b is greater or less than one.

A topic that sometimes arises in discussions of population growth is that of "doubling time." If a population continues to grow at its present rate of b, how long will it take for the population to double in size? To answer this question, suppose that the population doubles by the time $t*$; that is,

$$\frac{y_{t*}}{y_t} = \frac{ab^{t*}}{ab^t} = b^{t*-t} = 2 \tag{2.12}$$

To solve the above equation for $t* - t$, the time it takes the population to double at a constant growth rate b, we take the logarithm[6] of each side of equation (2.12).

$$(t^* - t)\, ln\, b = ln\, 2 \tag{2.13}$$

Dividing each side of the above equation by $ln\, b$,

$$t^* - t = ln\, 2 / ln\, b = 0.693 / ln\, b \tag{2.14}$$

From equation (2.14) we may determine the doubling time, $t - t^*$, given the growth rate b. To illustrate, some doubling times for selected growth rates are

Growth rate : (%/year)	1%	2%	3%	4%	5%	6%	7%
Doubling time : (years)	69.7	35.0	23.4	17.7	14.2	11.9	10.2

Thus, for example, a population growing at a constant rate of 5% per annum will double in size in just over 14 years ($ln2/lnb = ln2/ln1.05 = 14.2$).

Linear Transformation of the Exponential Function

In contrast to the case of the linear function, we cannot directly apply linear regression analysis to the non-linear exponential function to estimate values of the parameters a and b. As discussed in Appendix B, however, regression analysis can yet be of assistance if we first apply logarithms to construct a linear transformation of the non-linear function. Let us first express equation (2.7) in terms of population P_t at time t as

$$P_t = ab^t \tag{2.15}$$

Taking the natural logarithm of each side of equation (2.15), we have

$$ln\ P_t = ln\ a + (ln\ b)t \tag{2.16}$$

which we may write as the linear equation

$$P'_t = a' + b't \tag{2.17}$$

where $P'_t = ln\ P_t$ and the coefficients a' and b' are equal to ln a and ln b, respectively.

Estimates $\hat{a}'$ and $\hat{b}'$ of a' and b' can now be obtained through linear regression. A projected value of P_t, given t, can then be constructed by substituting the estimated coefficients into equation (2.17) and taking the antilogarithm of the resulting value of P'_t.

A Numerical Illustration

Suppose we have the following five observations of a growing population:

t:	0	1	2	3	4
P_t:	1,000	1,257	1,661	2,178	2,875
$P_t - P_{t-1}$:	–	31	42	56	73

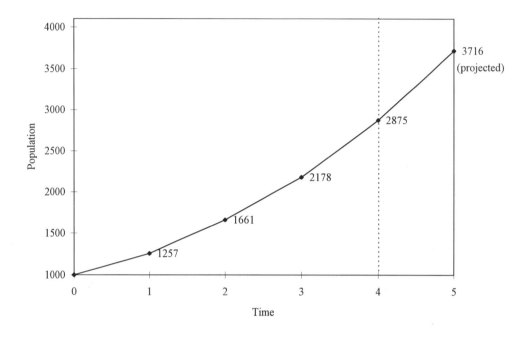

Figure 5. Exponential population growth

A review of the above increments of growth and of the graph of the data in Figure 5 for times 0–4 indicates that the growth pattern approximates an exponential growth path.

We now wish to fit the exponential function of equation (2.17) to the observations in order to project the population to $t = 5$. The first step is to find logarithms of the series of observed values (1,000, 1,257, ..., 2,875). We then regress the logarithmic values (6.9078, 7.1365, ..., 7.9638) against time (0, 1, ..., 4) in accordance with equation (2.17). The results are as follows:

Regression Output:

Constant	6.889523
Std Err of Y Est	0.012974
R Squared	0.998813
No. of Observations	5
Degrees of Freedom	3

X Coefficient(s)	0.266176
Std Error of Coeff.	0.005297

Regression Equation: $P'_t = 6.8895 + 0.2662t$

We may now calculate $P_5' = 6.8895 + 0.2662\,(5) = 8.2204$. Our projected population is thus $P_5 = \text{antiln}(P_5') = \text{antiln}\,(8.2204) = 3{,}716$, as shown in Figure 5.[7]

Polynomial Functions

A polynomial function is of the general form

$$y = a_0 + a_1 x + a_2 x^2 + a_3 x^3 + \dots + a_n x^n \tag{2.18}$$

A polynomial is said to be of the degree equal to the highest power present. For example, $y = 4x^2 - 6x + 25$ is a polynomial of the second degree. Depending on the degree, there are several classes of polynomial functions:

Degree	Polynomial	
zero	$y = a_0$	[*constant* function]
first	$y = a_0 + a_1 x$	[*linear* function]
second	$y = a_0 + a_1 x + a_2 x^2$	[*quadratic* function]
third	$y = a_0 + a_1 x + a_2 x^2 + a_3 x^3$	[*cubic* function]
etc.		

As seen from the above, a first-degree polynomial is a linear function, a second-degree polynomial is a quadratic function, and a third-degree polynomial is a cubic function. Quadratic and cubic functions are sometimes used in projections to produce a better fit with the data than that obtained by other functions. For example, if the population is expanding at an increasing rate, the quadratic function, which is capable of producing a pattern of growth similar to the exponential function but more concave (i.e., "bowed"), might be employed. Because the quadratic function can produce any portion of a U-shaped curve (upright or inverted) when fitted to a particular set of observations, it has the four possibilities shown in Figure 6.

Since both the exponential and quadratic functions may be used to make non-linear projections, the question arises as to how one makes a choice between the two functions. This matter is considered in Chapter 3, after all five of the mathematical functions have been described. Briefly, the most appropriate function to employ for projection purposes is the one that (a) best fits the historical data, and (b) best describes, in the analyst's judgment, the trend most likely to prevail in the future.

Linear Transformation of a Polynomial Function

To transform non-linear higher degree polynomial functions into linear functions, it is not necessary to use logarithms; one has only to transform the independent variables. For example, the quadratic function

$$P_t = a_0 + a_1 t + a_2 t^2 \tag{2.19}$$

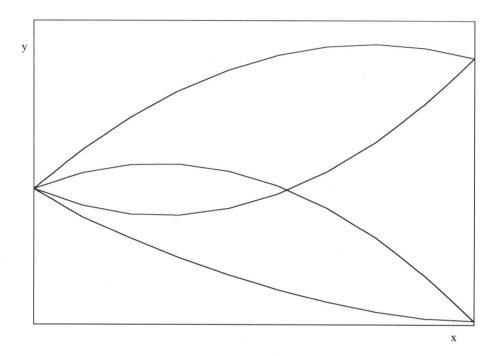

Figure 6. The quadratic function

can be expressed as a linear function

$$P_t = a_0 + a_1 t + a_2 z \qquad (2.20)$$

where z takes on the values of t^2. The dependent variable P_t can now be regressed on the independent variables t and z.

A Numerical Illustration

As an example of a polynomial applied to a set of observations of a population over time, let us use equation (2.20) of a quadratic function to project the following observations of a growing population:

t:	0	1	2	3	4
P_t:	1,000	1,057	1,335	1,773	2,301
$P_t - P_{t-1}$:	–	57	278	438	528

The values of z in the equation are the squares of the values of t: 0, 1, 4, 9, and 16. Using multiple regression, we can regress the values of P_t (1,000, 1,057, ..., 2,301) against the values of t (0, 1, ..., 4) and z (0, 1, ..., 16). The resulting estimates of the parameters a_0, a_1, and a_2 are 987.0, 16.9, and 78.7, respectively, as seen from the regression results below:

Regression Output:

Constant		987.0
Std Err of Y Est		29.302365
R Squared		0.998556
No. of Observations		5
Degrees of Freedom		2
X Coefficient(s)	16.94	78.71
Std Error of Coeff.	32.667303	7.831386

Regression Equation: $P_t = 987.0 + 16.9t + 78.7t^2$

We may now project population P_t at $t = 5$ as $P_5 = 987.0 + 16.9(5) + 78.7(25) = 3,040$. A graph of the population growth is shown in Figure 7.

The Hyperbolic Function

The hyperbolic function is a non-linear function that may be expressed as

$$y = a + \frac{b}{x} \tag{2.21}$$

As seen from Figure 8, the hyperbolic function approximates the exponential decay function when $b > 0$ and the modified exponential function (discussed in the next chapter) when $b < 0$. In both cases y approaches the limit a asymptotically as x increases.

Linear Transformation of the Hyperbolic Function

As was the case with the quadratic function, logarithms are unnecessary for the transformation of the non-linear hyperbolic function into a linear function. To convert the hyperbolic

$$P_t = a + \frac{b}{t} \tag{2.22}$$

to a linear form, one has only to rewrite the function as

$$P_t = a + b z \tag{2.23}$$

where z takes on the values of $1/t$. The dependent variable P_t can now be regressed on the independent variable z.

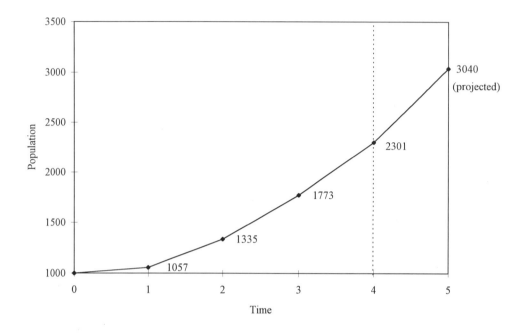

Figure 7. Quadratic population growth

A Numerical Example

As an example of a hyperbolic function applied to a set of observations of population over time, let us use equation (2.23) to project the following set of observations:

t:	1	2	3	4	5
P_t:	1,000	1,230	1,382	1,436	1,468
$P_t - P_{t-1}$:	–	230	152	56	32

A review of the incremental change in population from one observation to the next and of the graph of the data in Figure 9 suggests that the population is growing along a path traced by a hyperbolic function. (A guide to selecting functions in view of the observations of population changes over time is presented in Chapter 3.) The values of z are (1, 1/2, 1/3, 1/4, 1/5). The times of the observations begin with 1 rather than 0 in order to avoid the undefined mathematical operation 1/0. Regressing the values of P_t (1,000, 1,230, ..., 1,468) on z, we obtain the estimates

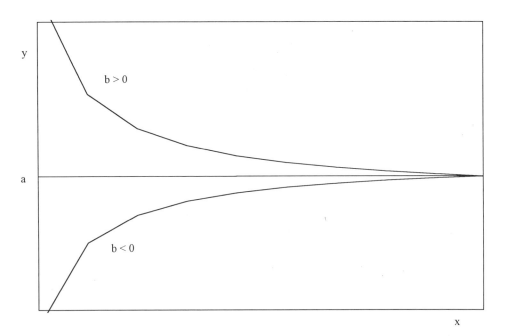

Figure 8. The hyperbolic function

of the parameters a and b as 1,571.6 and -587.7, respectively, as seen from the regression results below.

Regression Output:

Constant	1571.601
Std Err of Y Est	31.09952
R Squared	0.980434
No. of Observations	5
Degrees of Freedom	3

X Coefficient(s)	-587.74	
Std Error of Coeff.	47.93689	

Regression Equation: $P_t = 1571.6 - 587.7/t$

We may now project P_t at $t = 6$ as $P_6 = 1571.6 - 587.7 \,(1/6) = 1,474$.

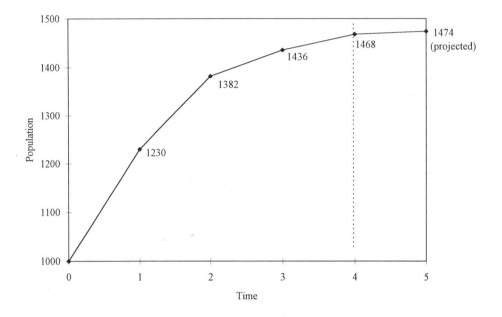

Figure 9. Hyperbolic population growth

Summary

Once counts or estimates of the magnitudes of past populations of an area have been established, a projection of the future size of the population may be constructed by extrapolating the trend, i.e., the relationship between population size and time as indicated by the data. Extrapolation of the trend defined by the observations may also be applied to data pertaining to other demographic phenomena such as births, deaths, and migration. One approach is to graph the past observations and to draw a curve, extending the curve over future time periods in a free-hand manner or with the aid of a drafting device.

An alternative means of extrapolation is to employ a mathematical function. For the purpose of extrapolating demographic trends in this manner, four basic mathematical functions were considered: linear, exponential, polynomial, and hyperbolic.[8]   Expanding populations following paths traced by these functions increase in constant absolute amounts (linear), at a constant rate (exponential), at a decreasing rate (hyperbolic), or at an increasing rate (quadratic). The appropriate conditions under which each of these functions is to be used for projection, and the means by which the analyst may choose among them, are discussed more fully in the following chapter.

Chapter 3

Mathematical Extrapolation II

The mathematical functions presented in the previous chapter trace growth paths without known upper limits. In this chapter we will consider a mathematical function, commonly used in demographic projections, that has a known upper (and lower) limit: the modified exponential.

The modified exponential function differs from the exponential in that there is an established upper (lower) bound on the population growth (decline). Over time the population is assumed to approach the boundary asymptotically, that is, at an ever-decreasing rate of change. A population to which the function is appropriately applied is one that has recognized environmentally or administratively established barriers to its continued expansion. An example of such a population might be that of a school district with firmly established areal boundaries and an upper bound on population density set by zoning regulations.

Chapter 3 also includes a summary review of all five mathematical functions and their linear transformations, where appropriate. Following this review, attention is turned toward the development of a four-step procedure for making projections. The procedure includes a set of guidelines for making a choice among the five functions in light of the trend of past observations.

The Modified Exponential Function

A population growing along a path traced by the modified exponential function is constrained in its expansion by an upper bound. This boundary or limit on the expansion of the population may be, for example, the result of geographical constraints. Alternatively, the population bound may be one imposed by planners intent on controlling growth.

Representing the bound as c, the modified exponential function may be written as

$$y = ab^x + c \qquad (3.1)$$

The function is similar in form to the exponential, save for the addition of the constant c. The precise path traced by the function depends on the values of the function's three parameters, a, b, and c. Graphs of the function with upper and lower bounds are shown in Figure 10.

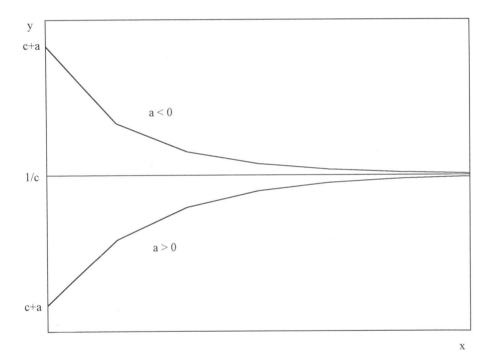

Figure 10. The modified exponential function

The growth curve in Figure 10, with c as an upper limit, is the form of the function that is frequently of interest to demographers. When x is zero, $b^x = 1$ and y is thus equal to $c + a$. Since a is a negative number (as shown in Figure 10), $(c + a) < c$. As x increases, b^x becomes progressively smaller, since b is a positive number less than one. Hence, y approaches c as b^x approaches zero. The smaller the value of b, the more rapidly y approaches c as x increases.

Linear Transformation of the Modified Exponential Function

As was the case with the exponential function, the parameters of the modified exponential function may be estimated by means of regression analysis once the function has been transformed into a linear form by means of logarithms.

Expressing equation (3.1) in terms of population P_t at time t, we may write

$$P_t = ab^t + c \qquad (3.2)$$

The first step in the transformation is to subtract the constant c from each side of equation (3.2). It is assumed that we are working with the growth function as shown in Figure 10, for which $a < 0$ and $b, c > 0$.

$$P_t - c = ab^t \quad (a < 0; \ b, c > 0) \qquad (3.3)$$

Given that $a < 0, b > 0$, and c is the positive upper bound of P_t, both sides of equation (3.3) are negative. Since logarithms of negative numbers are undefined, the second step is to multiply each side of the equation by -1 in order to make the expressions on both sides of the equation positive.

$$c - P_t = ab^t \quad (a, b, c > 0) \qquad (3.4)$$

Note that in equation (3.4) $a > 0$ in contrast to equation (3.3) in which $a < 0$. This change is the result of multiplying each side of equation (3.3) by -1. We may now take the logarithm of each side of equation (3.4).

$$ln(c - P_t) = ln\, a + (ln\, b)t \qquad (3.5)$$

Equation (3.5) may be rewritten in the familiar linear form of

$$P_t' = a' + b't \qquad (3.6)$$

where $P_t' = ln(c - P_t), a' = \ln a$ and $b' = \ln b$. Assuming c is known, y can be projected once estimates $\hat{a}'$ and $\hat{b}'$ are established through regression analysis.[1]

A Numerical Illustration

For the purpose of illustration, let us apply the modified exponential function to the five population observations (1000, 1203, 1382, 1436, 1468) presented in the numerical illustration of the hyperbolic function shown in Chapter 2. Let us suppose that because of existing residential zoning constraints, we may reasonably assume in the foreseeable future an approximate upper limit of 1,500 people in our subject area.

Our projection of population at $t = 5$ may now be constructed by means of the following steps:

1. Find the estimates $\hat{a}'$ and $\hat{b}'$ of the coefficients a' and b' of equation (3.6) by regressing P_t' against t, where $P_t' = ln(c - P_t)$. From the regression results shown below, $\hat{a}' = 6.229$ and $\hat{b}' = $ -0.6937.

Regression Output:

Constant	6.229123
Std Err of Y Est	0.056197
R Squared	0.998035
No. of Observations	5
Degrees of Freedom	3

X Coefficient(s)	-0.69373
Std Error of Coeff.	0.017771

Regression Equation: $P_t' = 6.2291 - 0.6937t$

2. Substitute $t = 5$ and the above estimates of a' and b' into equation (3.6) to find $P_5' = 6.229 - 0.6937 (5) = 2.7605$.

3. Since $P_5' = ln(c - P_5)$, take the antiln of 2.7605 to find that $c - P_5 = 15.8$.

4. Given that c has been estimated to be 1,500, our projected value of population at $t = 5$ can now be calculated as $P_5 = 1,500 - 15.8 = 1,484$.

The resulting population growth pattern is shown in Figure 11.

Mathematical Extrapolation: A Review

The steps to apply each of the five mathematical functions considered in the last two chapters for projections of populations are summarized below.

Linear: $P_t = a + bt$

1. Regress P_t against t to obtain the regression estimates $\hat{a}$ and $\hat{b}$.

2. Project to time t^* by means of the equation

$$P_{t^*} = \hat{a} + \hat{b}\, t^* \qquad (3.7)$$

Exponential: $P_t = ab^t$

1. Transform the exponential function into a linear function.

$$ln\, P_t = ln\, a + (ln\, b)\, t = a' + b'\, t \qquad (3.8)$$

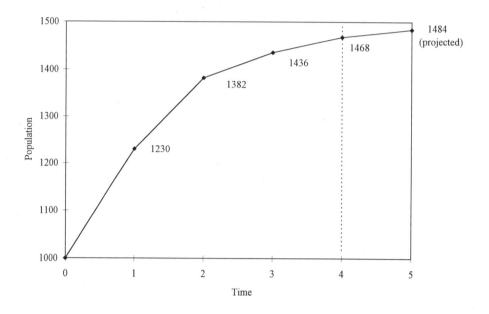

Figure 11. Modified exponential population growth

2. Regress $ln\,P_t$ against t to obtain the regression estimates $\hat{a}'$ and $\hat{b}'$.

3. Project to time t^* by means of the equation

$$P_{t*} = antiln[\hat{a}' + \hat{b}'\,t^*] \tag{3.9}$$

Quadratic: $P_t = a + b\,t + c\,t^2$

1. Transform the quadratic function into a linear function.

$$P_t = a + b\,t + c\,z \quad where\; z = t^2 \tag{3.10}$$

2. Regress P_t against t and z to obtain the regression estimates $\hat{a}, \hat{b}$ and $\hat{c}$.

3. Project to time t^* by means of the equation

$$P_{t*} = \hat{a} + \hat{b}\,t^* + \hat{c}\,t^{*2} \tag{3.11}$$

Hyperbolic: $P_t = a + \frac{b}{t}$

1. Transform the hyperbolic function into a linear function.

$$P_t = a + b z \quad where \; z = \frac{1}{t} \tag{3.12}$$

2. Regress P_t against z to obtain the regression estimates $\hat{a}$ and $\hat{b}$.

3. Project to time t^* by means of the equation

$$P_{t^*} = \hat{a} + \frac{\hat{b}}{t^*} \tag{3.13}$$

Modified Exponential: $P_t = a\, b^t + c$

Increasing function $(a < 0,\, 0 < b < 1,\, c > 0)$

1. Transform the modified exponential function into a linear function.

$$ln(c - P_t) = ln\, a + (ln\, b)\, t = a' + b' t \tag{3.14}$$

2. Regress $ln(c - P_t)$ against t to obtain the regression estimates $\hat{a}'$ and $\hat{b}'$.

3. Project to time t^* by means of the equation

$$P_{t^*} = c - antiln[\hat{a}' + \hat{b}' \, t^*] \tag{3.15}$$

Decreasing function $(a > 0,\, 0 < b < 1,\, c > 0)$

1. Transform the modified exponential function into a linear function.

$$ln(P_t - c) = ln\, a + (ln\, b)\, t = a' + b' t \tag{3.16}$$

2. Regress $ln(P_t - c)$ against t to obtain the regression estimates $\hat{a}'$ and $\hat{b}'$.

3. Project to time t^* by means of the equation

$$P_{t^*} = c + antiln[\hat{a}' + \hat{b}' \, t^*] \tag{3.17}$$

Choosing among Extrapolations

Once we have tabulated the observed historical values of a population (or of any other variable such as birth, death, or migration rates), how do we choose the appropriate mathematical function to project these values forward as a function of time? After reviewing the standard methods for calculating prediction errors, a recommended procedure for answering this question is presented.

Measuring the Prediction Error

As argued earlier, if no mathematical mistakes have been made by the analyst, a projection cannot be in error since it is merely the result of numerical calculations based on a specific set of assumptions. If, however, the projection is taken to be the predicted outcome at a particular point in time (future or past), the difference between the actual and predicted outcomes may be calculated as the "prediction error."

A common approach to choosing among projection techniques is to use available data to project to a known (census) year with each of the competing techniques and compare the resulting prediction errors, that is, the degree to which the predicted (projected) population deviates from the known population. Two common measures of this error are the mean squared error (MSE) and the mean absolute percentage error (MAPE). They are defined as follows:

$$MSE = \frac{1}{n} \sum_i (Y_i - Y_i')^2 \qquad (3.18)$$

$$MAPE = \frac{100}{n} \sum_i \frac{|Y_i - Y_i'|}{Y_i} \qquad (3.19)$$

where Y_i = the ith observed value of the dependent variable;
Y_i' = the ith predicted value of the
dependent variable; and
n = the number of observations.

Both the MSE and the MAPE are measures of the prediction error. The MSE is calculated by summing the squares of the differences between the observed and predicted values of the dependent variable and then dividing by the number of observations to obtain the mean. The differences are squared to avoid the addition of offsetting positive and negative values.

The MAPE is computed by first summing the differences between the observed and predicted values of the dependent variable. In this case, the summation of offsetting positive and negative differences is avoided by taking the absolute value of, rather than squaring, the differences. The sum is then divided by the number of observations to construct the average and multiplied by 100 to obtain the percentage.

For the purpose of illustrating the calculation of the MSE and the MAPE, let us "fit" a simple linear function to the local population data shown below; that is, let us use a linear equation, established through regression analysis, to project each of the five observed population values. From the regression equation of $P_t = 1,050 + 122.5\,t$ the estimated population values are:

t:	0	1	2	3	4
P_t (observed):	1,000	1,200	1,350	1,425	1,500
P_t (projected):	1,050	1,172	1,295	1,418	1,540

With the values of the observed populations and the projected populations considered as forecasts, we can proceed to calculate both the MSE and MAPE. The MSE is

$$[(1,000 - 1,050)^2 + (1,200 - 1,172)^2 + ... + (1,500 - 1,540)^2]/5 = 1,587.5$$

The MAPE is calculated as

$$100/5\,[|1,000 - 1,050|/1,000 + |1,200 - 1,172|/1,200$$

$$+... + |1,500 - 1,540|/1,500] = 2.91\%.$$

In the above illustration, the MSE and MAPE are used as measures of how well the linear function fits the observed data. These measures can then be compared with, say, those associated with mathematical functions such as the exponential, the quadratic, etc.

If population data are available for a number of regions or areas, the MSE and MAPE measures may be used to see which of several projection techniques produces the lowest prediction error over several data sets. That is, each projection technique is employed to project to a known (census) year for each of the areas. The technique's resulting prediction errors can then be averaged over all the areas and compared with the errors associated with competing projection techniques.[2]

In the discussion to follow, the MAPE is given preference over the MSE because of the more intuitive appeal of a percentage prediction error compared with a squared error.

A Four-Step Projection Procedure

For projecting a series of observations over time, a four-step procedure is shown in Figure 12. The observations that are to be projected over time may be of population, birth rates, death rates, migration, or any other variable of interest to the analyst. This procedure will be used repeatedly in the chapters to follow.

Step 1. Plot the observations on a graph.[3] If the pattern is obvious, extend the graph to the projection date. For example, if the observations clearly show a linear path, or if the values have become relatively constant over the last few periods, extend the graph to the projection date to obtain the projected value. If the pattern of the graphed observations is not obvious, proceed to Step 2.

Step 2. Select and graph two or more of the mathematical functions considered in this chapter for comparison with the graph of the observations. The following criteria

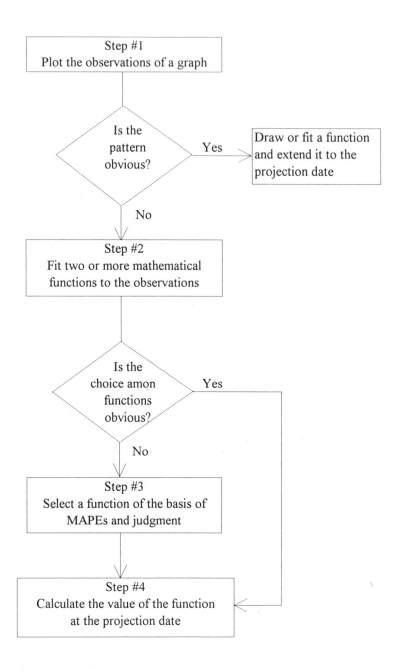

Figure 12. A four-step projection procedure

are intended to serve as an aid in the selection process.

(a) Dependent variable increasing over time in increments of:

– increasing size:

Exponential
Quadratic

– constant size:

Linear

– decreasing size:

Quadratic
Hyperbolic
Modified Exponential

(b) Dependent variable constant over time:

Linear

(c) Dependent variable decreasing over time in increments of:

– decreasing size:

Exponential
Quadratic
Hyperbolic
Modified Exponential

– constant size:

Linear

– increasing size:

Quadratic

Estimate the parameters of each function using regression analysis and plot the functions. (In cases in which the dependent variable is increasing or decreasing but the manner in which it is doing so is unclear, all five functions may be appropriately selected.) If the choice among the functions is obvious, go to Step 4. Otherwise, proceed to Step 3.

Step 3. Select a mathematical function on the basis of MAPEs and what you judge to be the most likely future value. (Employment of judgment in the selection of the appropriate mathematical function to be used for extrapolation is illustrated in examples presented in later chapters.)

Step 4. Calculate the value of the function at the projection date.

Summary

To the four mathematical functions (linear, exponential, polynomial, hyperbolic) discussed in Chapter 2, the present chapter adds another: the modified exponential. The modified exponential function differs from the previous four in that it assumes the existence of a known upper or lower bound. All five functions are commonly used to extrapolate observations of population and elements of population change (fertility, mortality, and migration). The extrapolation approach to projection is based on the assumption that the past relationship between these variables and time will continue into the future.

The principal advantages of the extrapolation approach to projection are that it is inexpensive and easily applied. Furthermore, there is ample empirical evidence (see Chapter 4) that, for projecting total population, extrapolation performs as well as, or better than, more sophisticated methods. If population size is the analyst's sole concern, the extrapolation of mathematical functions, selected by the four-step procedure outlined above, is likely to be the most cost-effective means of projection.

Used independently of other approaches to projection, however, mathematical extrapolation has significant potential limitations. Simply put, any future influence on the variable being projected that significantly differs from influences in the past will introduce a measure of error into the extrapolation. For example, phenomena such as the closing of a military base, the location of a manufacturing plant, a major alteration in the regional transportation system, or a substantial shift in the age structure of the population through migration are ignored by simple mathematical extrapolation. Selection based on the accuracy of the fit between the selected mathematical function and past observations will not ensure a comparable fit of the function to future dates.

Chapter 4

Comparative Methods

The purpose of this chapter is to add to our "toolbox" of projection techniques several comparative methods. Comparative methods of population projection differ from extrapolation methods in that they rely not only on past observations of the population under study, but also on the relation of the size of this population to that of another area. The two classes of comparative methods considered in this chapter are the "ratio" and "difference" methods.

Ratio methods are the most frequently applied of the comparative approaches to demographic projection. With these methods the population of interest, the "local" population, is projected as a ratio or share of a "parent" population, a larger population that includes the local population. Ratio methods rely on independent projections of the parent population, presumably produced with levels of resources and sophistication beyond those available at the local level.

Difference methods focus on the variation between the growth rates of the local and another population. The latter is generally, but not necessarily, a parent population. Projections of future differences between the growth rates of the two populations are made on the basis of past observations.

Although not considered further in this chapter, a third class of comparative methods might be termed "analog" methods. Generally applied informally, analog methods involve the projection of the population of one area on the basis of another, generally older, area which is judged to possess similar social and economic characteristics. This latter area is termed the "reference" area. The growth path of the local population is assumed to follow the growth path of the reference area. The latter path may serve as a guide in the selection of a mathematical function to extrapolate the size of the local population. The population of the reference area may or may not be a parent of the local population.

Ratio Methods

Ratio or share methods focus on the relationship of the local population to a parent population. For the purpose of projecting the local population, the analyst may either assume this relationship to be constant or attempt to project the relationship on the basis of past observations.

The basic equation of ratio methods is

$$P_{t+1} = k P'_{t+1} \qquad (4.1)$$

where P_t is the local population, P'_t is the population of the reference area, and k is a constant which describes the relationship between the two populations, as shown in Figure 13.

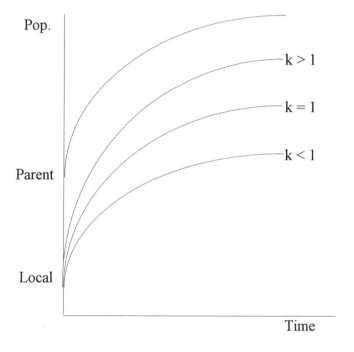

Figure 13. Local and parent population growth

Constant Share Method

With the constant share method of projection, the future local population is assumed to be the same proportion of a larger, parent population that it was at the last observation. Illustrative examples of situations in which this approach might be appropriately applied are the population of a small area as a part of a larger municipal population, a municipal population as a share of the population of the inclusive metropolitan region, or a metropolitan population as part of its parent provincial or state population.

The constant share model may be stated algebraically as

$$P_{t+1} = kP'_{t+1} \tag{4.2}$$

where $k = P_t/P'_t$ and is assumed to be constant over the period of analysis.

For the purpose of providing numerical illustrations of the constant share method as well as other projection methods in this chapter, let us assume the following observations over five periods for the local population P_t and the parent population P'_t, as shown below:

t:	1	2	3	4	5
P_t:	1,000	1,200	1,350	1,425	1,500
$P't$:	10,000	13,000	15,000	16,000	17,000

With the constant share method, as expressed in equation (4.2), all that is needed to project the local population to time 6 are the data at time 5 and the projected parent population. Assuming P'_6 has been projected to be 17,500 by analysts directly concerned with the parent population, the projection of the local population to time 6 produced by the constant share model is $P_6 = (1,500/17,000)$ $17,500 = 1,544$.

Projected Share Methods

Projected share methods are dependent not only on exogenous projections of the parent population but also on the projection of changes in the local population's share of the parent population.[1] That is, the k in equation (4.1) represents not the present share of local population but a projected future share. There are, of course, a variety of ways in which the local population's share of the parent population may be projected. One simple method for doing so is to assume that the ratio of the local to parent population in the next time period will be equal to the average of, say, the previous three observations; that is,

$$P_{t+1} = kP'_{t+1} \tag{4.3}$$

where $k = [(P_t/P'_t + P_{t-1}/P'_{t-1} + P_{t-2}/P'_{t-2})/3]P'_{t+1}$

From our hypothetical data, the projection of the local population to period 6 by means of equation (4.3) is $P_6 = [(1,500/17,000 + 1,425/16,000 + 1,350/15,000)/3]$ $17,500 = 1,559$.

In calculating the average in equation (4.3), each of the three observed ratios of local to parent population is equally weighted. Such weighting does not take into account the obvious upward trend in the data. When a trend is apparent, it is desirable to assign relatively greater weights to the more recent years.[2] For example, we might weight each annual growth rate twice as heavily as the preceding rate. Since the weights must sum to one, they would be in our three-period example 4/7, 2/7, and 1/7. With these weights our projected population would be $P_6 = [(1,500/17,000)(4/7) + (1,425/16,000)(2/7) + (1,350/15,000)(1/7)]\ 17,500 = 1,552$.

An alternative to projecting the share of the local population on the basis of a calculated average is to apply regression analysis. This may be done by any one of the mathematical functions shown in the previous two chapters. That is, in accordance with the four-step procedure of Chapter 3, we examine the observations (and the graph) of k, the population share, and decide on the basis of inspection and judgment or by comparing MAPEs which function (linear, exponential, hyperbolic, polynomial, or modified exponential) to fit to the data. The share may then be mathematically extrapolated, as previously discussed. The basic equation is

$$P_{t+1} = kP'_{t+1} \tag{4.4}$$

where $k = (P/P')_{t+1}$ and the immediate task is to find the future share $(P/P')_{t+1}$ through simple linear regression.

From our hypothetical data, the ratio of local to parent population is:

t:	1	2	3	4	5
k_t:	.1000	.0923	.0900	.0891	.0882

Our procedure resulted in the selection of the hyperbolic function. (The exponential decay and quadratic functions were rejected on the basis of a visual inspection of their fits to the above values and their higher MAPEs.) The regression results for the hyperbolic function are shown below:

Regression Output:

Constant	0.085215
Std Err of Y Est	0.000202
R Squared	0.998657
No. of Observations	5
Degrees of Freedom	3
X Coefficient(s)	0.014685
Std Error of Coeff.	0.000311

From the above regression data, we may calculate k_6, the value of the ratio of local to parent population projected to time 6, as $0.0852 + 0.0147/6 = 0.0877$. Our projected local population from equation (4.4) is thus $P_6 = 0.0877\,(17,500) = 1,534$.

Difference Methods

Unlike share methods, which focus on the local share of the parent population, difference models are concerned with the variance between the growth rates of the two populations.

Constant Difference Method

The underlying assumption of the constant difference model is that the future growth rate differential between the local and parent populations will be identical to that of the last observed period; that is,

$$\frac{P_{t+1}}{P_t} - \frac{P'_{t+1}}{P'_t} = \frac{P_t}{P_{t-1}} - \frac{P'_t}{P'_{t-1}} \tag{4.5}$$

where P and P' again represent the local and parent populations, respectively. Solving equation (4.5) for the projected local population,

$$P_{t+1} = \left(\frac{P_t}{P_{t-1}} + \frac{P'_{t+1}}{P'_t} - \frac{P'_t}{P'_{t-1}}\right) P_t \tag{4.6}$$

Retaining the assumption of the previous section that the parent population projected to period five is 17,500, we may apply the constant difference model of equation (4.6) to our illustrative data to obtain a projection of the future local population: $P_6 = (1,500/1425 + 17,500/17,000 - 17,000/16,000)\,1,500 = 1,529$.

Projected Difference Method

The projected and constant difference models differ in the same way as do the projected and constant share models. In the projected difference model the variation between the growth rates of the local and parent populations is projected into the future based on observations of past differences. This projection may be undertaken by applying linear regression.

As a first step in formulating the model we may express the difference in growth rates d in period t as

$$d_t = \frac{P_t}{P_{t-1}} - \frac{P'_t}{P'_{t-1}} \tag{4.7}$$

Local population is then projected to time $t + 1$ as

$$P_{t+1} = (d_{t+1} + \frac{P'_{t+1}}{P'_t}) \, P_t \qquad (4.8)$$

where d_{t+1} is found via regression analysis.

From our data the differences between the growth rates of the local and parent populations are as shown below:

t:	1	2	3	4	5
d:	–	-.1000	-.0288	-.0111	-.0099

An inspection of the growth rate differences leads to the judgment that the downward trend levels off at 0.01. Assuming that the difference in growth rates between the local and parent population continues at this limit, the projected value of the local population at time 5 from equation (4.8) is determined as $P_5 = 1,500 \, (0.01 + 17,500 \, / \, 17,000) = 1,559$.

Choosing among Methods

A number of projection methods have been considered in this chapter. When applied to our five hypothetical observations, each yields a different value for the projection to time six. Two questions thus arise. How does one choose among the various comparative methods? How does one choose between comparative and extrapolation methods?

The choice in each of the two cases should be based primarily on how well the various methods have performed in the past with regard to the study area of concern. The projection methods that have performed best in the past are the obvious candidates for use in projecting to the future. In most cases, however, track records for a wide range of the various techniques discussed are likely not to exist and will have to be created. If the currently desired projection is for x years, then it is the task of the analyst to use past observations to project x years forward to a past year for which the population size is known. This exercise is undertaken for each of a number of extrapolation and comparative methods. The relative performances of the methods can then be judged by their associated MAPEs.

A less preferable approach to making a choice among methods is to consider their relative performances in other geographic areas. An example of a study which offers such a basis for comparison is that of Isserman (1977). Because the study was restricted to a limited number of comparative methods,[3] its results are arguably more relevant to the question of choosing between extrapolation and comparative methods than they are to that of choosing among comparative methods.

On the basis of 1930–70 census data for 1,579 Illinois townships, Isserman prepared a number of projections using ten readily constructed extrapolation and comparative methods shown in Table 1.

Table 1. Projection methods and their associated errors

Method	Acronym	Description	MAPE
Extrapolation Methods:			
Linear	LINAVE	Pop. change = average change over past observations	11.5
	LINREG	Regression of pop. against time	11.8
Exponential	EXAVE	Pop. change = average rate of change over past observations	11.1
	EXREG	Regression of logarithm of pop. against time	10.8
Double logarithmic	DLOG	Regression of logarithm of pop. against logarithm of time	11.3
Comparative Methods:			
Constant share	CONSH	Share of county pop. = last observed share	13.1
Linear share	LINSH	Regression of share of county pop. against time	13.0
Exponential share	EXPSH	Regression of ln of share of county pop. against time	11.0
Constant difference	CONDIF	Difference between township and county growth rates = last observed difference	13.3
Linear difference	LINDIF	Regression of difference against time	17.7

Source: Adapted from Isserman 1977: 249, 251.

Data for the period 1930–50 were used to project the total population of each township to 1960 and data from 1930–60 were used to project 1970 populations.

Regarding the projections as forecasts and comparing the projections with the known population counts of 1960 and 1970, MAPEs were taken as a measure of the prediction errors.

The results are shown in Tables 1 and 2.[4]   Among Isserman's (1987:251) principal findings, as can readily be seen from the results, were that the comparative methods considered in the study were generally less accurate than were the non-comparative, extrapolation methods.[5]   Overall, the comparative methods did not perform as well as did the simpler, extrapolation techniques. This evidence supports the conclusion reached by Greenberg et al. that "despite their obvious shortcomings, extrapolation methods are the simplest and probably the most cost-effective means of making short-term minor civil division projections."[6]

Table 2. Percentage distribution of forecast errors, 1960-70

Error	0–0.74	0.75–0.89	0.90–1.09	1.10–1.24	1.25+
LINREG	8.5	23.7	55.8	10.5	1.5
LINAVE	7.9	22.7	56.8	11.1	1.5
EXREG	3.7	18.2	59.6	14.9	3.5
EXAVE	3.2	17.0	59.2	16.4	4.2
DLOG	4.6	17.1	57.5	16.7	4.1
CONSH	3.8	10.2	53.3	22.8	9.9
LINSH	3.8	10.2	53.3	22.8	9.9
EXPSH	3.7	17.7	58.2	15.9	4.4
CONDIF	5.5	19.4	53.9	13.8	7.3
LINDIF	11.1	22.5	44.0	13.0	9.4

Source: Isserman. 1977: 252.

Summary

Comparative methods of demographic projections for a local area require projections or forecasts of an external, related population. The two types of comparative methods considered in this chapter are the ratio and difference methods. With ratio methods, and generally with difference methods, the external population is a parent population, i.e., a larger population inclusive of the local population.

When ratio methods are adopted, it is either assumed that the future local share of the designated parent population will be identical to the present share (constant share method) or an attempt is made to project the change in the local share (projected share method). Difference methods focus on the deviation of the local population growth rate from that of the parent population. In the application of these methods, it is either assumed that this deviation will be unchanged over time (constant difference method) or an attempt is made to project the change in the deviation (projected difference method).

With either the constant share or constant difference methods, an accurate prediction of the parent population may still result in an inaccurate prediction of the local population if the relationship between the two populations changes from that observed in the past. For this reason, efforts are frequently made to project the changing local share of the parent population (or difference between the growth rates of the two populations). Such projections may be undertaken by means of the four-step procedure discussed in the previous chapter.

While comparative methods have an intuitive appeal as projection techniques, the empirical results reviewed for projections of population size do not provide a sound basis for this appeal. Convincing empirical evidence of the superiority of these methods in this context over the mathematical extrapolation methods of the previous chapters has yet to be presented. Comparative methods are likely to be of greater value in projecting birth and death rates in cases in which the methods can provide local analysts with the benefits of the greater resources and expertise associated with projections at a parent level.

Chapter 5

The Cohort-Survival Population Model

Unlike the preceding mathematical extrapolation and comparative methods of projection, the cohort-survival model is designed to yield projections of the *composition* of the future population in addition to its size. The model is used to project a population disaggregated into cohorts (i.e., population segments) of uniform age and sex.

While population size is important to planning agencies, so generally is the composition of the population. For example, a population that is constant in size but changing in age composition can have significant implications for the provision of public services. The use of many such services (e.g., education, health and welfare, recreation, transportation) are in varying degrees age-specific. Various forms of medical services are sex-specific as well. Accurate assessments of the composition of future populations are also important to a wide range of private-sector commercial activities (e.g., housing, clothing, entertainment, and printing and publishing).

Of the three elements in the basic demographic equation—births, deaths and migration—the cohort-survival model deals explicitly with the first two. For this reason the focus of this chapter will be on the definitions of birth and death rates, their relevance to the cohort-survival model, and the fundamental considerations to be made in the projections of these rates. A review and discussion of techniques for the estimation of past rates of migration and the projection of future rates is the subject matter of the following chapter.

A fourth demographic process, one that is not included in the basic demographic equation, is that of aging. A unique feature of the cohort-survivor model is its explicit consideration of the aging process. Even a population with constant

44

birth and death rates and no in- or out-migration would likely find its age composition changing as its surviving members in each age group proceed over time into the succeeding age group.

The Basic Cohort Model

A simple numerical illustration of the application of a cohort-survival model to project a region's population is presented in this section, followed by an algebraic summary.

A Numerical Illustration

Let us consider a population of 848 persons composed of 420 males and 428 females. The population is divided into eight age groups, with the number of females exceeding males by one person in each of the groups. The numbers in this example are entirely arbitrary and have no bearing on the projection procedure.

Table 3 contains a simple cohort-survival model of a hypothetical society. The cohorts are disaggregated by sex. For example, in the initial or baseline population of Table 3, there are 60 males in the 20-29 age group and 61 females. Although cohorts are generally composed of five-year age groups, ten-year groups have been used in the model to simplify the exposition. There is, however, one exception to the ten-year grouping: the last cohort for each sex, cohort #8 in Table 3, includes all members of the sex-specific population 70 years and older. The number of years the population is to be projected is determined by the size of the age groups. For example, if the age groups are of five-year increments, the population may be projected 5, 10, 15,...years into the future.

Ignoring migration, cohort-by-cohort projection of the hypothetical population of Table 3 one period (ten years) into the future is undertaken in three basic steps. First, a projection of cohort #1 is made for each sex. The procedure is to calculate from the model all births occurring to the fertile female cohorts. In the population represented in Table 3, the fertile cohorts are the female cohorts #2–5. The number of births to each cohort is simply the number of women in the cohort times the cohort birth rate. For example, the number of births occurring over the ten-year projection period to women in the 20–31 age group, cohort #3, is determined as 61 x 1.50. The proportion of total births that are male is then determined by multiplying the number of births by 0.51, the ratio of male births to total births, as shown in Table 3. The female proportion is accordingly 1 - 0.51 = 0.49.

Table 3. A cohort-survival model of a hypothetical population

		Baseline population: Time 0				
Cohort	Cohort age	Cohort numbers		Survival rates		Birth rates
		Male	Female	Male	Female	
1	0–9	40	41	0.99	0.99	
2	10–19	50	51	0.97	0.99	0.05
3	20–29	60	61	0.95	0.97	1.50
4	30–39	70	71	0.93	0.95	0.40
5	40–49	65	66	0.91	0.93	0.01
6	50–59	55	56	0.89	0.91	
7	60–69	45	46	0.87	0.89	
8	70+	35	36	0.80	0.82	
Total		420	428			

Proportion of male births = 0.51

		Projected population: Time 1			
Cohort	Cohort age	Cohort numbers			
		Male		Female	
1	0–9	63	*	60	***
2	10–19	40	(40 x .99)	41	(41 x .99)
3	20–29	49	(50 x .97)	50	(51 x .99)
4	30–39	57	(60 x .95)	59	(61 x .97)
5	40–49	65	(70 x .93)	67	(71 x .95)
6	50–59	59	(65 x .91)	61	(66 x .93)
7	60–69	49	(55 x .89)	51	(56 x .91)
8	70+	67	**	70	****
Total		448		461	

*[(51x.05) + (61x1.50) + (71x.40) + (66x.01)] x .51 = 63
**(45x.87) + (35x.80) = 67
***[(51x.05) + (61x1.50) + (71x.40) + (.66x.01)] x .49 = 60
****(46x.89) + (36x.82) = 70

The second step in projecting the population is to project cohorts #2–7. For each cohort this is done by determining from the model how many persons of the previous age group survived to move into the next cohort during the projection period. For example, to project the number of males in the 10–19 age group in the next period, it is necessary to multiply the number of males in the 0–9 age group, 40, by the ten-year survival rate for the cohort, 0.99.

The last cohort to be projected is the 70+ age group. This is done in two steps.

First, one determines how many persons survived from the 60–69 age group—the same procedure that was used for cohorts #2–7. For cohort #8, however, one must add to this figure the number of persons in this cohort that survived over the ten-year period and thus remained in the cohort. For example, the projection of the population of female cohort #8 in the next period would be (46 x 0.89) + (36 x 0.82) = 70, as shown in Table 3.

The projected total population at time $t+1$ is the sum of the projected sixteen cohorts. Without taking migration into account, the population of both males and females in the model is seen to increase. For each sex the number of births exceeds the number of deaths over the projection period.

An Algebraic Summary

To summarize the cohort-survival model mathematically,[1] let us assume a hypothetical population divided into n male and n female cohorts. For each sex all cohorts except the last consist of the sex-specific population of an age group of m years. We now wish to describe algebraically the $2n$ population cohorts projected m years into the future. As was seen in the above example, it is the first and last cohort for each sex that must be given special attention.

Let us adopt the following notation:

M_i, F_i = male cohort i and female cohort i, respectively;
MS_i, FS_i = survival rates for male cohort i and female cohort i, respectively;
BR_i = birth rate for female cohort i; and
PM = proportion of male births.

We may define the cohorts projected m years into the future as:

$$M_1 = PM \ x \ \sum_{i=1}^{n} F_i \ x \ BR_i \qquad (5.1)$$

$$F_1 = (1 - PM) \ x \ \sum_{i=1}^{n} F_i \ x \ BR_i$$

$$M_2 = M_1 \ x \ MS_1 \qquad (5.2)$$
$$F_2 = F_1 \ x \ FS_1$$

$$\vdots$$

$$M_{n-1} = M_{n-2} \ x \ MS_{n-2} \qquad (5.3)$$
$$F_{n-1} = F_{n-2} \ x \ FS_{n-2}$$

$$M_n = \sum_{i=n-1}^{n} M_i \ x \ MS_i \qquad (5.4)$$

$$F_n = \sum_{i=n-1}^{n} F_i \ x \ FS_i$$

Mortality

Basic Measures

Mortality indices are frequently constructed for intertemporal and interspatial comparisons. By convention, the basic measures are indicators of the incidence of death occurring over a year to the population measured at the midpoint of the year. The interval of a year is generally adopted as the standard interval in order to avoid adjustments for seasonal influences on the death rate. Of the three mortality rates considered (crude, age-specific, and infant), the age-specific death rate is of particular relevance to the cohort-survival model, as it corresponds to the model's survivor rates.

Crude Death Rate (CDR)

The CDR is the most widely used and easily understood measure of mortality. It is defined as the number of deaths per thousand people over a one-year period, regardless of age or sex.

$$CDR = (\text{deaths / population at mid-year}) \ x \ 1000 \qquad (5.5)$$

The mid-year population is adopted as an approximation to the average number of people during the year who are "at risk" (that is, subject in this case to the possibility of death). The CDR is a 'crude' rate in that it does not take into account the influence of either age or sex on the death rate. Because of this deficiency, the measure is of limited usefulness in comparisons of mortality rates either over time or across space.[2]

From Table 4, the crude death rate is determined as

$$CDR = \frac{5,522 + 4,996}{677,580 + 703,160} \ x \ 1000 = 7.6 \qquad (5.6)$$

Table 4. Demographic data of a hypothetical metropolitan area

Age	Males	Females	Live births	Male deaths	Female deaths
0-1	11,430	10,885		74	79
1-4	35,275	33,115		15	18
5-9	41,965	39,900		6	9
10-14	41,615	39,870		12	7
15-19	48,095	46,080	688	40	12
20-24	58,955	59,865	3,897	71	23
25-29	64,695	66,675	7,607	77	30
30-34	62,220	63,030	5,397	81	32
35-39	59,570	59,975	1,769	92	50
40-44	47,055	45,990	170	115	67
45-49	38,380	37,635	11	142	72
50-54	35,445	33,840		236	110
55-59	34,175	33,735		356	182
60-64	30,215	34,110		472	293
65-69	23,995	30,220		571	402
70-74	19,830	26,340		775	564
75-79	12,840	18,850		797	668
80-84	7,265	12,075		714	726
85-89	3,135	6,795		488	802
90+	1,425	4,085		388	850
Total	677,580	703,160	19,539	5,522	4,996

In the above illustrative cohort-survival model, a survival rate is listed for each of the age and sex cohorts. A cohort survival rate is approximately equal to one minus the cohort mortality rate. In considering mortality rates further, we shall broaden the discussion to include not only cohort rates but a few of the more commonly applied measures.[3] A numerical illustration of each measure is presented, based on the demographic data of a hypothetical metropolitan area shown in Table 4.

Age-Specific Death Rates (ASDR)

An age-specific death rate for a population cohort is customarily defined as the number of deaths over a one-year period per thousand members of the cohort.

$$ASDR = (\text{deaths / population of cohort at mid-year}) \times 1000 \qquad (5.7)$$

From Table 4, the age-specific death rates for, say, males and females in the 20-24 age group are determined as

$$ASDR_{Males20-24} = \frac{71}{58,955} \, x \, 1000 = 1.2 \tag{5.8}$$

$$ASDR_{Females20-24} = \frac{23}{59,865} \, x \, 1000 = 0.4 \tag{5.9}$$

Age-specific survival rates (ASSR) utilized by the cohort-survival model based on five-year cohorts can be approximated from the ASDRs as[4]

$$ASSR_{Males20-24} = 1 - 5 \, x \, \frac{ASDR_{Males20-24}}{1000} = .9940 \tag{5.10}$$

$$ASSR_{Females20-24} = 1 - 5 \, x \, \frac{ASDR_{Females20-24}}{1000} = .9981 \tag{5.11}$$

Because the convention in the cohort-survival model is to define five-year cohorts in accordance with quinquennial censuses, each one-year ASDR used in the above calculations of ASSRs must be multiplied by five to obtain the total deaths over a five-year period.

Infant Mortality Rate (IMR)

The IMR is frequently adopted as an indicator of the general health and medical standards of a population. It is conventionally defined as the number of deaths of infants less than one-year old per thousand of live births.

$$IMR = (\text{deaths, 0–1 year of age / live births}) \, x \, 1000 \tag{5.12}$$

From Table 4 it can be seen that 74 males and 79 females died prior to reaching age 1. The infant mortality rate is thus calculated as

$$IMR = \frac{74 + 79}{19,539} \, x \, 1000 = 7.8 \tag{5.13}$$

It is to be noted that the denominator in the above ratio does not measure the population at risk in this case, since some of the infants who died during the year may have been born in the previous year. For this reason the IMR differs from an age-specific death rate for a population cohort of 0–1 years. The latter rate would substitute for live births in the above equation, the number of infants in the 0–1 age group. Thus, the ASDR for this age group would be calculated as $(74 + 79) / (11,430 + 10,885) \, x \, 1000 = 6.9$.

Projecting Death Rates

Death rates can be projected by constructing trends from past observations according to our four-step projection procedure of Chapter 3. Such projections are generally made on the basis of age-specific rates.[5] For example, suppose we had the following observations of the death rates (d.r.) of male cohorts aged 40-44:

t :	1	2	3	4	5	6	7	8
death rate:	4.72	3.97	3.22	3.82	2.99	3.47	3.01	2.87

t:	9	10	11	12	13	14	15	16
death rate:	2.58	2.59	2.54	2.05	2.44	2.22	1.97	2.49

We may now employ our four-step procedure to project the above age-specific death rate to time 20.

Step 1. Plot the observations.
A graph of the 16 observations appears in Figure 14.

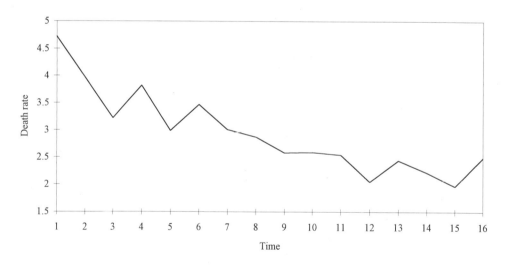

Figure 14. Observations of death rates

Step 2. Select and graph appropriate mathematical functions.
    The dependent variable is decreasing over time at what appear to be increments of decreasing size. The curve turns upward between observations 15 and 16, but our general knowledge of steadily increasing improvements in health care, in society's general knowledge of nutrition, in declining rates of smoking, etc., leads us to

the assumption that the observation at $t = 16$ is an aberration and that the trend will continue downward.[6] From our four-step projection procedure guidelines, we add to the graph of the observations the following functions: exponential, quadratic, hyperbolic, and modified exponential (with a limit from visual inspection of, say, 1.85). (See Figure 15.)

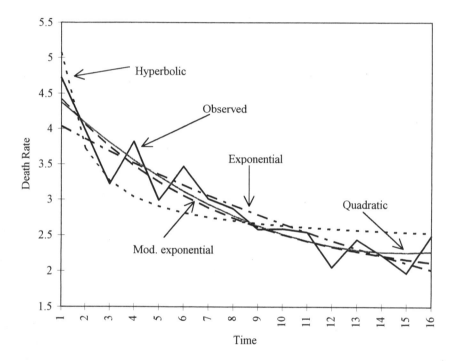

Figure 15. Mathematical functions fitted to observations of death rates

Step 3. Choose the mathematical function.

From the graph in Figure 15, there is no obvious choice among the five mathematical functions. Further, it is presumed in this case that the analyst has no basis for making a choice among the functions on the basis of expectations of how the trend in observed death rates will behave in the future. The analyst thus proceeds to calculate MAPEs.

Function:	*MAPE:*
Exponential	7.725
Quadratic	7.368
Hyperbolic	9.809
Modified Exponential	7.439

Although the quadratic function has the lowest associated MAPE, the function has reached its low point at time 15 and has begun to turn upward. Since it has been presumed that the upward turn in the observations over the period 15–16 is an aberration, the quadratic function is rejected and the modified exponential function with the next lowest MAPE is chosen to make the projection.

Step 4. Calculate the value of the function at the projection date.

The death rate of males aged 40-44 in our hypothetical locality projected to time 20 is calculated as

$$ASDR_{Males40-44} = 1.85 - antiln(1.0963 - 0.1518 \, x \, 20) = 1.99 \qquad (5.14)$$

where 1.85 is the assumed lower boundary and 1.0963, 0.1518 are the estimated coefficients of the modified exponential function (see Chapter 3) determined by regression analysis in Step 2.[7]

The future course of mortality rates continues to be the focus of much research and speculation among demographers. The virtual eradication of many communicable and infectious diseases in the Western world has brought heart disease and cancer to the fore as the principal causes of death. If epidemics attributable to continuing concerns such as warfare, AIDS, and environmental destruction can be avoided, a steady, gradual decline of mortality rates can reasonably be expected to result from advances in medical technology and trends toward more healthy lifestyles.

Fertility

Fertility refers to reproductive performance and is customarily measured in terms of live births. Similar to mortality, there are a number of measures of population fertility. The most frequently employed of these measures are briefly reviewed below. Of particular importance to the cohort-survival model are the age-specific birth rates.

Basic Measures

Crude Birth Rate (CBR)

Parallel with the crude death rate, the CBR is likely the most commonly applied measure of fertility. It is defined as the number of live births in a year per total population, preferably measured at mid-year.

$$CBR = (\text{births} / \text{mid-year population}) \times 1000 \tag{5.15}$$

The CBR is a 'crude' measure in the same sense that the crude death rate is so designated: both measures ignore the influence of age and sex. This lack of refinement is relatively dramatic in the case of the CBR. In the case of the crude *death* rate, age and sex determine the probability of death, but all members of the population are at risk. With regard to the CBR, whose denominator includes men and women of all ages, it may reasonably be expected that age and sex will exclude much more than half of the population from the possibility of bearing children. For this reason the CBR is of limited usefulness in comparing fertility rates between populations.

From Table 4, the crude birth rate of the hypothetical metropolitan area is determined as

$$CBR = \frac{19,539}{677,580 + 703,160} \, x \, 1000 = 14.2 \tag{5.16}$$

Age-Specific Birth Rate (ASBR)

The ASBR, or age-specific birth rate, for a particular female cohort i is defined as the number of live births occurring to the cohort in the course of a year.

$$ASBR_i = (\text{births to cohort } i / \text{mid-year cohort } i \text{ pop.}) \times 1000 \tag{5.17}$$

From Table 4, the age-specific birth rates for three of the seven fertile age groups are

$$ASBR_{15-19} = \frac{688}{46,080} \, x \, 1000 = 14.9 \tag{5.18}$$

$$ASBR_{20-24} = \frac{3897}{59,865} \, x \, 1000 = 65.1 \tag{5.19}$$

$$\vdots$$

$$ASBR_{45-49} = \frac{11}{37,635} \, x \, 1000 = 0.3 \tag{5.20}$$

For purposes of the cohort-survival model, the cohort rates are generally calculated over five-year intervals for females aged 15–49. Similar to the treatment of the age-specific death rate, each ASBR, because it is calculated in terms of births per year, must be multiplied by five (and divided by 1,000) to obtain the number of births over the five-year period. It is the latter figure which is required by the cohort-survival model in making projections in five-year increments.

General Fertility Rate (GFR)

The GFR is defined as the number of live births in a year per thousand women of child-bearing age in the population.

$$GFR = \text{(births / mid-year female pop. 15–49)} \times 1000 \qquad (5.21)$$

The denominator is sometimes taken to be the number of females aged 15–44 because of the small proportion of births attributable to women in the 45–49 age group. In such instances the relatively few births occurring to women over 45 are included in the births occurring to the 40–44 age group.

From Table 4, the general fertility rate is calculated on the basis of the female cohorts in the 15-19 through the 45-49 age groups.

$$GFR = \frac{19,539}{46,080 + 59,865 + \ldots + 37,635} \; x \; 1000 = 51.5 \qquad (5.22)$$

Because the GFR takes into account the influence of age and sex in determining births, it is a more useful measure than the CBR for comparing fertility rates between populations. It suffers, however, from the lack of accounting for the proportions of females within the various age groups between 15 and 49. The fertility rates of women aged 20–29, for example, are significantly higher than those for women in the 15–19 and 30–49 age groups. Both for comparison purposes and for implementation of the cohort-survival model, additional refinement with respect to age is needed.

Total Fertility Rate (TFR)

For the purpose of comparing fertility measures between populations it is cumbersome to have to deal with the several ASBR rates. To avoid this problem, demographers have constructed a single measure, the total fertility rate, which is an aggregation of the age-specific rates.

$$TFR = 5 \left(\sum_{i=15-19}^{i=40-49} ASBR_i \right) / 1000 \qquad (5.23)$$

The TFR is the number of children the "average" woman can be expected to have during her reproductive years.

To obtain the TFR figure, the ASBRs are first summed over the six five-year age cohorts. Since each ASBR is expressed as an annual average over a five-year interval, the result is then multiplied by five to obtain the number of births occurring over the reproductive period. The product is then divided by one thousand, since the TFR, in contrast to the ASBRs, is expressed in terms of one woman rather than a thousand women. The result is the number of children a typical woman in the population can be expected to bear as she passes through the ages of 15 to 49.[8]

From Table 4, the total fertility rate is calculated from the seven ASBRs as

$$TFR = 5\,x\,(14.9 + 65.1 + ... + 0.3)/1000 = 1.6 \qquad (5.24)$$

Projecting Birth Rates

The number of births in a population is a function of two factors: the number of females of child-bearing age (15–49) and the fertility of these women. The cohort-survival model can be used to project the numbers of fertile females in the population. As was the case with death rates, birth rates can be projected on the basis of our four-step projection model.[9] For example, suppose we had the following observations on the birth rates of female cohorts aged 20-25:

t:	1	2	3	4	5	6	7	8
b.r.:	134.65	122.71	122.55	116.86	119.46	115.22	108.69	106.30
t:	9	10	11	12	13	14	15	16
b.r.:	107.75	110.00	110.52	110.07	110.22	111.33	115.12	113.94

Let us now employ our four-step procedure to project the above age-specific birth rate to time 20.

Step 1. Plot the observations.
A graph of the 16 observations appears in Figure 16.
Step 2. Select and graph appropriate mathematical functions.
Although seven of the last eight observations reveal a rising trend, it might well be assumed by the analyst that this is temporary and that expected economic conditions and a continued increasing female participation rate in the labour force will cause the rate to decrease over the next few years. In contrast to the example of projecting age-specific death rates, the last observation is seen in this case not as an aberration but as a return to the longer term trend of decline. Support for this assumption might likely have come from an examination of trends in other areas or from the application of comparative methods to a parent population. Consistent with his or her expectation of a continued long-term decline, the analyst chooses to add to the graph of observations the following functions: exponential, quadratic,

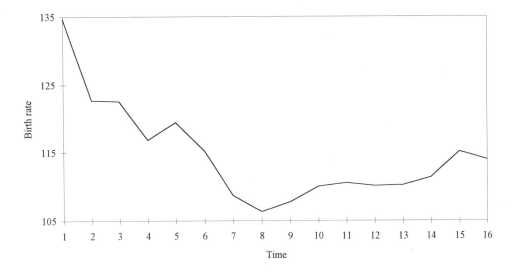

Figure 16. Observations of birth rates

and hyperbolic. Unwilling to hazard an estimate of a lower limit, the modified exponential function is foregone (see Figure 17).

Step 3. Choose the mathematical function.

From the graph in Figure 17, the hyperbolic function is chosen as being generally consistent with the analyst's expectations. The calculation of MAPEs is foregone.

Step 4. Calculate the value of the function at the projection date.

The birth rate of females aged 25-29 in our hypothetical locality projected to time 20 is calculated as

$$ASBR_{Females25-29} = 108.9830 + 27.1130 \,/\, 20 = 110.3 \qquad (5.25)$$

where 108.9830 and 27.1130 are the estimated coefficients of the hyperbolic function determined by regression analysis in Step 2.

Compared with death rates and with changes in total population over time, birth rates are relatively volatile. In deciding the general trend of the rates in the above illustration, the analyst based the decision on assumed economic conditions and rising female participation rates. Over the long run a number of other factors might be considered. For example, Day lists the following developments that appear in his judgment to render birth rates in Western societies "less subject

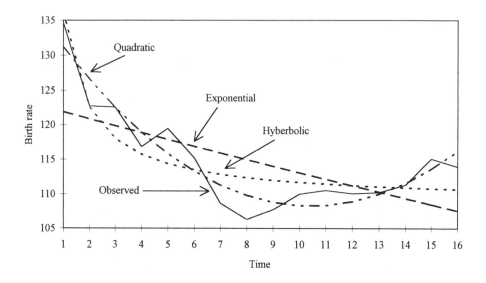

Figure 17. Mathematical functions fitted to observations of birth rates

to the fads and factors that, in the past, occasioned major fluctuations in annual numbers of births."[10]

1. A greater openness and frankness about human sexuality, which is likely to lead to greater knowledge and practice of birth control.

2. A wider range of available roles for women (other than mother and home-maker), particularly in the form of employment opportunities outside the home.[11]

3. Changes in attitudes relating to what is considered an "appropriate" family size.[12]

4. A narrowing of the range of actual family sizes with a particularly negative influence on those tending to large families.

5. Intentional concentration of childbearing within a narrower age range,[13] re-sulting in a shorter duration of childbearing, partly through shorter intervals between successive births and partly through fewer births altogether.

A similar grouping of interdependent influences on fertility in Canadian society has been delineated by Statistics Canada (1984a): the status of women in society, marriage and divorce, family size preferences, and the status of children in society.

To these factors might be added the availability of inexpensive, safe, and socially acceptable birth-control devices.[14]

Summary

In contrast to the previous chapters, which focused on projecting the *size* of future populations, the cohort-survival model is a component approach that results in projections not only of the size of the population[15] but of the age and sex distribution as well. The initial sex-specific age cohorts are projected using the population of the female cohorts of the child-bearing years, age-specific birth rates, and the proportions of male and female births. Cohorts for all other age groups, save the last, are projected by multiplying the previous period population by the cohort's survival rate. Projection of the population of the cohorts of the last age group is taken as the sum of the survivors of this group and the survivors of the previous age category (who have now aged into the last category).[16]

Death and birth rates may be projected using the four-step projection procedure of Chapter 3. Compared with projecting age-specific death rates as required by the cohort-survival model, the task of projecting birth rates is considerably more difficult. While death rates can be expected to continue to be correlated with the progress of biomedical research and environmental change, they are likely to continue to be significantly less volatile than birth rates, which remain subject to a number of varying influences such as marriage and divorce rates, female labour force participation rates, family size preferences, and the acceptability and availability of contraceptive devices.

For most regions, however, variations in both birth and death rates are relatively small in comparison with those in migration rates.

Chapter 6

Migration Models

Of the fundamental demographic processes of natural increase and migration, it is frequently the latter that is the major contributor to population changes at the regional and small-area levels. Because of their importance, migration flows have long been of primary concern to demographic analysts. As early as the late nineteenth century, Ravenstein[1] set forth several basic 'laws' of migration based on his analysis of data from England and other nations.

1. The volume of migration from area A to area B decreases with the the distance between the two areas.

2. Urban expansion exerts a step-by-step impact extending to the hinterlands. Newly created jobs in the city are taken by people living close to the city. The jobs that are left by these migrants are in turn taken by people in the more remote hinterlands.

3. To every stream of migration there is a counterstream.

4. The propensity to migrate is lower among urban populations than it is among rural populations.

5. Females tend to outnumber males in short-distance migrations.

6. Technological development, in that it increases economic activity or improves transportation, tends to stimulate migration.

7. Among the many determinants of migration, economic factors overwhelmingly predominate.

More than a century of study of the process of migration has generated considerable support for Ravenstein's findings. With continued technological progress in transportation and communications, migration remains of primary importance in demographic analysis, and research in the area continues to expand. Difficulties in undertaking such research, however, persist. Unfortunately for the analyst concerned with migration flows, time-series data are generally not available. Moreover, migration rates are extremely volatile over time compared with birth and death rates and are therefore relatively difficult to predict.

In this chapter some fundamental concepts regarding migration are briefly reviewed prior to considering methods of estimating past migration streams and projecting future flows.

Basic Concepts

In parallel with our previous discussions of mortality and fertility, there are a number of basic concepts and measures pertaining to migration that are standard in the demographic and forecasting literature. Knowledge of these elements is necessary to the task of empirically estimating past, and projecting future, migration flows.

Immigration and Emigration

A legal immigrant is a person who has acquired landing, that is, lawful permission to come into a country with the intention of establishing permanent residence. An emigrant is one who transfers his or her permanent residence from one country to another. While North American and European federal governments keep records on immigrant visas and the countries in which applications are made, comparable data for emigration are generally not available.[2]

In-Migration and Out-Migration

The terms "in-migration" and "out-migration" are used to distinguish purely *internal* flows of migration from immigration and emigration. Not every internal transfer of residence can, of course, be appropriately classified as contributing to a migratory stream. What is considered as migration and what is dismissed as merely a "move" will depend on the nature of the study, but migration generally involves a transfer of residence across an administrative boundary, while a move occurs within the jurisdiction.

For a particular study area, transfers of residences may thus be divided into three categories:

- moves—changes of residence within the boundaries of the study area.

- internal migration—changes of residence that cross study area boundaries but occur within national boundaries.

- international migration—changes of residence that cross both study area and national boundaries.

From these categories it is evident that the distinction between local movement and migration depends on the defined area. Areal boundaries are set in each case by the analyst according to the nature and focus of the study. In- and out-migration are then determined by changes of residences across these boundaries, as seen in Figure 18. If, for example, the area of study is a municipality, then transfers of residence across municipal boundaries constitute migration, while residential changes within the municipality would be considered local moves. Local moves do not affect the area's population, only its spatial distribution.

Gross and Net Migration

Gross migration refers to the *sum* of migration flows crossing study area boundaries in both directions. It is a measure of total population "turnover" for the jurisdiction under study. Gross migration at the national level is the sum of immigration and emigration; at the subnational level, it is the sum of in-migration and out-migration. The subnational flows may contain both a domestic and international component.

Net migration is the *difference* between the two directional streams. It is the volume of people transferring their residences into the area minus the volume of people permanently leaving. Positive net migration expands the local population; negative net migration diminishes it. A net migration of zero produces no impact on the size of the population of the study area. If the in- and out-migration flows are significant, however, even though they are off-setting in magnitude they will likely have an impact on the characteristics of the population; that is, the change in age, sex, and ethnic patterns may be substantial and have significant implications for the future size and composition of the population.

> A focus on gross instead of net migration flows more clearly identifies the patterns, illuminates the dynamics, and enhances the understanding of demographic processes that occur in multiple interacting populations. Distinguishing between flows and changes in stocks reveals patterns that otherwise may be obscured; focusing on flows into and out of a regional population exposes dynamics that otherwise may be hidden; and linking explanatory hypotheses to appropriately disaggregated gross flows permits a more accurately specified projection model.[3]

Unfortunately, data problems frequently compel the demographic analyst to forgo estimates of gross migration streams and focus solely on net migration.[4]

Figure 18. In- and out-migration

Migration rates indicate the relative frequency with which the migration event occurs. At the subnational level, four such rates may be defined as

In-migration rate: I/P   Gross migration rate: $(I + O)/P$
Out-migration rate: O/P   Net migration rate: $(I - O)/P$

where I and O represent in-migration and out-migration, respectively, and P is the average or mid-interval population.

Causes of Migration

The motivations for individuals and households to migrate domestically (and internationally) may be conceptually grouped in terms of 'pushes' from the sending area and 'pulls' from the receiving area. For example, a person who has recently lost a job may feel a push from the area to seek work elsewhere. Someone seeking post-secondary education may experience a pull into an area in which a desirable university is located. For many migrants a variety of push and pull factors may be operating, and it may be difficult to ascertain which are predominant. Such factors may include:[5]

Push Factors:

1. Decline in a national resource or in the prices paid for it; decreased demand for a particular product or the services of a particular industry; exhaustion of mines, timber, or agricultural resources.

2. Loss of employment resulting from being discharged, from a decline in need for a particular activity, or from mechanization or automation of tasks previously performed by more labour-intensive procedures.

3. Oppressive or repressive discriminatory treatment because of political, religious, or ethnic origins or membership.

4. Alienation from a community because one no longer subscribes to prevailing beliefs, customs, or mode of behaviour—either within one's family or within the community.

5. Retreat from a community because it offers no or few opportunities for personal development, employment, or marriage.

6. Retreat from a community because of catastrophe—flood, fire, drought, earthquake, or epidemic.

Pull Factors:

1. Superior opportunities for employment in one's occupation or opportunities to enter a preferred occupation.

2. Opportunities to earn a larger income.

3. Opportunities to obtain desired specialized education or training, such as a college education.

4. Preferable environment and living conditions—climate, housing, schools, other community facilities.

5. Dependency—movement of other persons to whom one is related or betrothed, such as the movement of dependents with a breadwinner or migration of one marriage partner to join the other.

6. Lure of new or different activities, environments, or people, such as the cultural, intellectual, or recreational activities that a large metropolis might offer to rural and small-town residents.

In addition to these push and pull factors, there is between every origin and destination a set of intervening obstacles. These obstacles include the financial and psychological costs of transporting one's residence. Further, there may exist between the origin and any potential destination a number of competing "opportunities" (e.g., employment possibilities, environmental amenities, the residences of family and friends). These competing opportunities add to the complexity of the decision-making process regarding migration and, consequently, to the task of modelling this process.

Finally, one may consider also the personal factor, that is, the reactions of potential migrants to the preceding influences. Each individual is likely to value differently the positive and negative factors at the present and prospective locations, as well as the intervening obstacles and competing opportunities between the locations.[6] In part, these differences in valuations may be attributable to differences in life-cycle stages. For example, a good school system may be valued highly by parents who appreciate the educational opportunities afforded their children, negatively by childless home-owners who focus on the property taxes necessary to support the schools, and with indifference by renters without children. Differences between individual valuations also depend on personalities, which may range from a favourable disposition with regard to change to one of extreme resistance.

In sum, these four elements—positive and negative factors associated with the area of origin, positive and negative factors associated with the area of destination, intervening obstacles and competing opportunities, and personal factors—yield insight into the potential complexity of constructing behavioural models of migration.[7] The variety of factors influencing the migration process is discussed further in this chapter in a later section on projecting future migration.

Estimating Past Migration

Establishing the magnitudes of past migration streams is frequently critical to projecting future streams more accurately. For the purpose of estimating internal migration the data problem is severe.[8]   There is nothing in North America resembling "population registers," such as those in Scandinavia, China, and Japan, which require citizens to record changes in place of residence. Accordingly, there are no directly generated and complete records with regard to internal migration. Past and current migration streams must be estimated.

There are currently two fundamental approaches to constructing estimates of past migration flows: direct estimation on the basis of data pertaining to place of residence and indirect estimation via a 'residuals' method.

Direct Estimation of Migration

In the direct estimation approach, both in- and out-migration flows are estimated by the use of place-oriented data such as telephone installations, hydro connections, and government records (e.g., driver's licences, property tax billings, and voter registrations).[9]   There are problems that are fairly common to all such data. To illustrate with respect to telephone installations, errors may readily occur in the estimation of both in- and out-migration because of the fact that not every individual has a phone registration in his or her name. For example, a new installation may result from a resident in the locality who formerly did not appear in the telephone company records. Such would be the case when young adults in the locality acquire their first phones. Regarding such a new installation as indicative of in-migration would lead to an overestimate of the in-migration process.

On the other hand, in-migration is underestimated by this approach to the extent that in-migrants do not appear on telephone installation records over the period of analysis. This circumstance would occur if the in-migrants move into residences in which there is no change in phone registration (e.g., homes of friends or families of the in-migrants, group homes, and boarding houses) or if, during the period of analysis, the in-migrants do not apply for telephone service.

Similar problems arise with respect to estimating out-migration on the basis of utility records. For example, the cessation of service by persons without application of new service elsewhere in the locality is not necessarily indicative of out-migration. Such circumstances may be attributable to household mergers and to deaths, thus leading to overestimation of the out-migration process. The process tends to be underestimated, however, to the extent that out-migration occurs among those residents who were not previously recorded on the telephone company's books.

Indirect Estimation of Migration

The alternative to estimating in- and out-migration directly on the basis of data pertaining to place of residence, such as utility records, is to estimate net migration indirectly as a residual. This is done by relying on population enumerations from consecutive census years and estimating migration from the modified basic demographic equation (1.1) of Chapter 1:

$$(IM - OM) = (P_1 - P_0) - (B - D) \qquad (6.1)$$

Net Migration = Population Change – Natural Increase

where $(IM - OM)$ = net migration (in-migration - outmigration)
over the period 0 to 1;
B = births over the period;
D = deaths over the period; and
P_1, P_0 = population at times 1 and 0, respectively.

Suppose, for example, that population from the last census was 1,000, which amounted to an increase over the count of 800 recorded in the previous census. If net natural increase in the intercensus period is estimated as 70, net migration into the area can then be calculated as a residual by means of equation (6.1): (1,000 – 800) – 70 = 130.

Two basic residual methods are the vital statistics method and the cohort-survival approach to migration estimation. Unlike the direct estimation approach based on place-oriented data, both residual procedures attempt to estimate net migration rather than the separate flows of in-migration and out-migration.

The Vital Statistics Method

While no data directly pertaining to internal migration are kept, there are available, at the local level, highly reliable data with respect to births and deaths. With the population counts from the census years, these vital statistics data may be used in equation (6.1) to estimate net migration into the area. There are some difficulties with this approach, however.[10]

Perhaps the potentially most significant source of estimation error is the difference in the undercount rates in the two census years. If, for example, the percentage undercount is lower in the later census year, residual net migration over the intercensal period would be overestimated.

Changes in the boundaries of the region under study between the two census years will also distort the migration estimate. If annexation and consolidation have occurred in the region in the intervening period, residual migration will be overestimated unless appropriate adjustments are made to achieve geographic conformity between the initial and terminal census populations.

Other possible difficulties include the treatment of special components of the population, such as military personnel, and the allocation to place of residence of the enumerated populations and recorded births and deaths.

As discussed in the preceding section, the vital statistics method yields a single figure for net migration. If, however, the census data are assembled on an age and sex basis, and vital statistics pertaining to the local area are available on a similar basis, then the net migration process can be estimated by age and sex cohorts.

The Cohort-Survival Method

The cohort-survival method of estimating net migration is based on the population projection model of the same name (discussed in Chapter 5). The logic of the approach is straightforward. Assuming five-year censuses, each age and sex cohort of census year $t - 5$ is projected to census year t on the basis of the birth and survival rates established in the cohort-survival model. The resulting population estimate for period t is then compared with the census count of that year. The difference between the two figures is the resulting estimate of net migration into or from the local area over the five-year period.[11]

The cohort-survival approach is specifically designed to estimate the net migration stream by age and sex cohort. As such, it may be either a complement to, or a substitute for, the vital statistics method. If the census data and the vital statistics data are both available on an age and sex basis, then the two approaches yield comparable estimations.

Inaccuracies of the birth and survival rates aside, the cohort-survival method, like the vital statistics method, is subject to such various practical problems as adjusting for differential rates of census undercounts, accounting for boundary changes, and dealing with special components of the local population (e.g., military personnel and college students).

Projecting Future Migration

The literature relating to migration studies is considerably diverse.[12] This diversity is attributable in large part to the varying viewpoints and foci of the disciplines that have addressed the nature and underlying determinants of the process. For example, while economists tend to stress the expectations of altered conditions of income and employment associated with anticipated changes of residences, psychologists are generally more concerned with the rationality and nature of the decision-making process. Geographers are prone to give primary emphasis to the spatial aspects of migration.

On the whole, however, there is an abundance of empirical evidence (in accordance with Ravenstein's 'laws') that suggests economic opportunities are a dominant underlying motivation for interurban and rural-urban migration. In light of this evidence, it is clear that migration into a particular area depends not only on the economic health of the area but also on economic conditions within other areas, particularly those that have served historically as sources of in-migration and those that have been traditional destinations of the area's out-migrants. Unfortunately, at the local level the resources required to undertake such analyses generally exceed those available.

It is also unfortunate that the complexity of the migration process is likely to continue to expand over time rather than diminish. As economic globalization proceeds, it forces upon local areas an increasing variety of direct and indirect economic influences and related structural adjustments. Added to these sources of economic uncertainty are environmental factors, which are becoming increasingly important in the migration process.[13]   Moreover, the environment's role is likely to expand over the long run, since various environmental changes (e.g., resource depletion, shifting climatic conditions) will increasingly translate into economic change and uncertainty.

Two broadly defined approaches to projecting future migration employed by urban planners and geographers are briefly discussed below.[14]   The first consists of the extrapolation of past estimates of migration on the basis of the projection techniques discussed in earlier chapters. The second approach is based on regression analyses that attempt to infuse behavioural content into the projection process, primarily by focusing on the economic determinants of migration decisions.

Extrapolation of Past Trends

In view of the difficulties and uncertainties associated with the projection of future migration streams and the limited resources most planning agencies have to devote to the task, it is not surprising that planning analysts frequently turn to simply projecting past trends.[15]   (However, for even this relatively elementary operation to be undertaken, past trends must have been established by residual methods or some other means.)

As another illustration of our four-step projection procedure, let us assume that a residual method has been employed to produce the following eight estimates of past net migration flows:

t:	1	2	3	4	5	6	7	8
Migr.:	6543	6610	6829	7284	7530	8271	8642	9492

Let us now employ our procedure to project the above migration flows to time 9.

Step 1. Plot the observations.
A graph of the 8 observations appears in Figure 19.

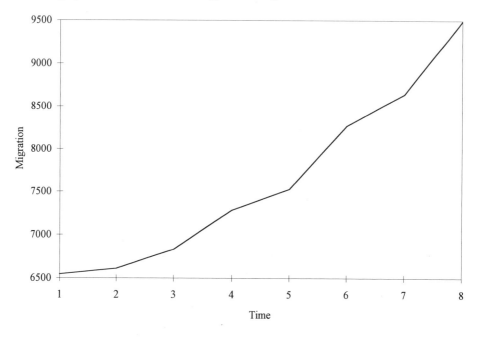

Figure 19. Observations of migration flows

Step 2. Select and graph appropriate mathematical functions.
The above plot of the past estimates of net migration into the local area reveals migration to be increasing in increments of increasing size. From our guide in Chapter 3, we select the exponential and quadratic functions to fit to the data.

Step 3. It appears from the graph that the quadratic function ($P_t = a + bt + ct^2$) provides the better fit. This observation is confirmed by the calculation of MAPEs: exponential: 2.01; quadratic: 0.90. The quadratic provides a greater concavity or "bend" compared to the exponential.

Step 4. Migration at time 9 is calculated to be 6439 + 17.89 (9) + 43.79 (81) = 10,147. The constant and slope coefficients were obtained from the regression equation constructed in Step 2.

In some instances, the adoption of the ratio methods of Chapter 4 may prove to be a more useful approach to the problem. This is particularly the case if migration

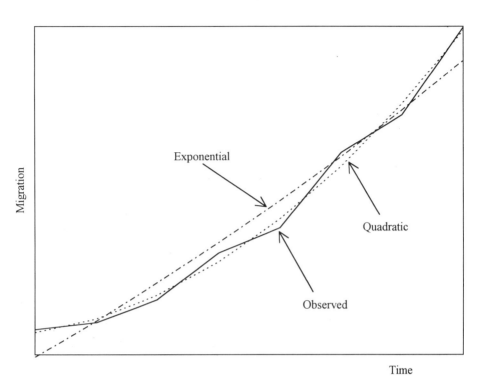

Figure 20. Mathematical functions fitted to observations of migration flows

is overwhelmingly from outside the 'parent' area. The ratio approach would also assume that the senior level of government responsible for the projection or forecast of the parent population has allocated an appropriate level of resources for the analysis of changing economic conditions and has accordingly produced projections or forecasts of future migration for the larger area based on this analysis. Under these conditions, projection of net migration associated with the local area as a share of the parent stream will to some extent indirectly account for changing economic conditions. The analyst would still be left, however, with the task of projecting the smaller component of migration into, and from, the local area *within* the 'parent' area.

In making migration projections, it is not uncommon for the analyst to take two additional steps. First, to the information regarding past trends, the analyst may add his or her specific knowledge of local economic conditions, particularly the outlook for commercial and industrial residential construction. Information regarding commercial and industrial expansion plans, building and construction permits, zoning changes, planned subdivisions, etc., pertains directly to the migration estimation process. This information may be used to shape the projection of future migration either through the analyst's judgment or, more formally, as inputs to a quantitative modelling process based on, say, multiple regression analysis.

A second step frequently undertaken is the preparation of more than one projection of migration. Typically, these multiple projections consist of "high" and "low" values or of "high," "low," and "medium" figures. (In accordance with the discussion in Chapter 1, if the analyst is willing to label one of the projections a "best-guess," that particular projection becomes a forecast.) Different scenarios and policy recommendations associated with each projection may then be developed.

Regression Models

For at least the past three decades, empirical studies of migration, net or gross, have been dominated by multiple regression models.[16]   This dominance can be attributed to two factors: the scarcity of time series data on migration flows and the lack of behavioural content of mathematical extrapolation methods. Migration flows result from push and pull factors such as those listed earlier in this chapter, and projections and forecasts of migration are thus undertaken in reference to these factors. The regression approach to modelling migration provides the analyst with the flexibility of utilizing a range of determining, or explanatory, variables.[17] Two types of regression models are briefly considered below: unidirectional and bidirectional.   Unidirectional regression models focus on the identification of statistically significant determinants of migration under the assumption that the migration process itself does not, in turn, affect the determining factors; bidirectional regression models relax this assumption and explicitly recognize "feedback" possibilities which alter the migration flows.

Regression: Unidirectional Models

The majority of regression models of migration are unidirectional, single-equation models in which migration appears only on the left-hand side of the equation as the dependent variable. The independent, causal variables on the right-hand side of the regression equations are selected from a range of demographic, economic, and psychological variables but generally emphasize the economic.[18]

For analysts undertaking regression analyses of the determinants of migration, empirical measures of the factors discussed in this chapter must be established. Examples of such measures used in migration regression models are shown in Table 5.

Table 5. Determinants of Canadian intermetropolitan migration

Variable	Empirical measure
Labour market component	
Earnings opportunities	Industrial wage composite;
Employment opportunities	Ind. composite emp. growth
Unemployment	Unemployment rate
The business cycle	Residential building construction
Government transfers	
Unemployment insurance	UIC benefits; availability
Government fiscal policy	Federal transfers to provinces
Natural resource revenues	Resource revenues
Additional economic factors	
Home ownership	Ownership, 25–34 year-olds
Housing costs	Cost of new housing units
Dual income-earning households	Female labour force participation
Immigration	Immigration of foreign born
Information and psychic costs	
Distance	Distance
Language	Commonality of language
Social and amenity considerations	
Crime	Crimes of violence
Climate severity	Total snowfall
Selectivity considerations	
Education	Proportion of highly educated

Source: Adapted from Shaw, R.P. 1985. *Intermetropolitan Migration in Canada.* Ottawa: Supply and Services, 90.

Regression: Bidirectional Models

While the major share of regression models of migration can be categorized as unidirectional models, the migration process in some cases clearly generates actions that, in turn, have an impact on the migration process itself. These feedback effects can be illustrated by the simple diagram in Figure 21.

As represented in the figure, the migration process is determined by the supply and demand of labour. If the demand for labour in the area exceeds the supply, the area will experience in-migration. If supply exceeds demand, out-migration is presumed to result. The migration process, in turn, influences both the supply and demand for labour. For example, suppose there is in-migration into the area.

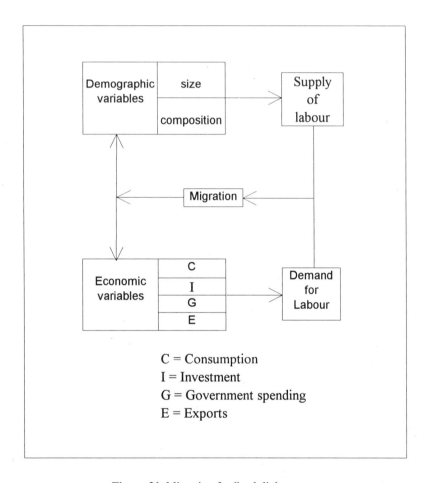

Figure 21. Migration feedback linkages

With an unchanged labour participation rate, the supply of labour in the area will be increased via an expanded population. The labour supply may also be affected through influences on the participation rate via demographic components such as age, sex, and ethnicity. Further, if the levels of education and work experience of the migrants differ from those of the resident population, the quality of the labour supply may be altered as well.

As shown in Figure 14, migration also affects the demand for labour. For example, increased migration will increase consumption spending in the area. Investment expenditures in the area may also increase via residential lot servicing and construction. To the extent that the in-migrants have an entrepreneurial orientation, investment expenditures may rise via the capital the newcomers bring with them or through the capital funds that they borrow. Further, government spending (e.g., spending on public facilities and social services) and transfers (e.g., per-capita grants) can be expected to increase as the area's population level expands. Finally, over the long run, increases in export sales of business activities created by in-migrants may also increase the demand for labour.

Not included in the diagram are other influences on the migration process, such as government policy (e.g., relocation subsidies) and environmental conditions (e.g., clean air, accessibility). The migration process may generate feedback effects through these influences as well. The longer the period of population projection, the greater is the rationale for considering the bidirectional economic-demographic model.[19]

In view of the difficulties and resources required for clearly establishing the feedback linkages in bidirectional models as well as the underlying determinants of the migration process in unidirectional models, there are a number of analysts who are of the opinion that sophisticated econometric models for the purpose of projecting internal migration are not cost effective, at least for most municipal planning offices.[20] As stated earlier, this is particularly the case for projections of total population.[21]

In his assessment of the state of constructing economic-demographic models for population forecasting, Simmons (1981:84) concludes that

> simple trend lines appear to do as well as complex equation systems, and the combination of national demographic trends, recent demo-graphic history, and projected economic growth include the most rel-evant characteristics ... More accurate population projections must incorporate projections of the local economy. Although the relation-ship between job creation and net migration is imperfect, it is still the strongest relationship that is available. In general, simple projection models based on a small number of variables will do as well as more complex schemes.

The issue of the appropriate level of simplicity to be applied to the demo-graphic modelling effort at the local level is not one on which there is considerable agreement. The appropriate model will depend on the needs of those who use the model's results and on the resources available to the analyst.

Summary

Migration occurs when principal residences have been transferred across specified boundaries. The underlying causes of migration are varied. A partial list may be compiled by grouping factors that result in a 'push' from the area of origin and those that contribute to a 'pull' to a particular area of destination. To this list may be added the many barriers (and competing alternatives) to transferring residences between the two areas, as well as a variety of personal factors that lead to differences in individual valuations of the relevant factors.

In order to project future migration streams more accurately, the empirical estimation of past migration flows is frequently necessary in order to obtain some notion of the magnitudes of these streams. When appropriate data relating to the place of residence (e.g., telephone installations, hydro connections, government administrative records) are available, direct methods of estimating past migration flows can be employed. An alternative to the use of public records to estimate net migration is to adopt an indirect, 'residuals' approach, based either on vital statistics or the cohort-survival methods of estimation. In this approach, the first step is to estimate the local population in the latest census year solely on the basis of the reproductive change from the previous census year. This is done on the basis of vital statistics gathered for the locality or by using the cohort-survival model, with its birth and survival rates. The resulting estimate is then subtracted from the census year estimate to obtain net migration as a residual.

The projection of future migration streams can be undertaken by our four-step procedure. An alternative approach is to construct a regression model that incorporates as explanatory variables empirical measures of what the analyst believes to be the principal underlying determinants of the migration process under study. While a wide range of demographic, psychological, and economic variables have been specified as determinants in regression models of migration flows, the variables have generally been economic in nature. The vast majority of these "economic-demographic" models have been unidirectional; that is, migration appears only as a dependent variable and is thus presumed to exert a negligible influence on its determining factors. There is, however, a gradually increasing amount of empirical work focusing on bidirectional economic-demographic models that attempts to explicitly incorporate the feedback effects of the migration process.

Chapter 7

A Final Note

Four approaches to demographic projections were considered in the preceding chapters: mathematical extrapolation, comparative methods, cohort-survival, and multiple regression models focusing on migration flows. In this chapter the relative advantages and appropriate applications of each of these approaches are reviewed.

Mathematical Extrapolation

Mathematical extrapolation involves the projection of observed magnitudes of a past demographic phenomenon (e.g., population levels, birth rates, death rates, and migration flows) into the future by selecting a mathematical function to fit to the data. Five primary functions that are frequently used in demography were considered in this text: linear, exponential, quadratic (polynomial), hyperbolic, and modified exponential. Illustrative applications of these functions were given. Any number of other functions can be similarly applied, of course, such as the power function (Appendix B) and the logistic and Gompertz functions (similarly S-shaped functions), which frequently appear in the demographic literature.[1]

Application of the mathematical extrapolation approach is recommended to be undertaken in a four-step procedure: (1) plot the observations on a graph; (2) select and graph two or more of the functions in accordance with the guidelines presented in Chapter 3; (3) choose a mathematical function that either conforms to judgment regarding the likely future behaviour of the demographic variable under consideration or results in the lowest associated MAPE; and (4) calculate the value of the function at the targeted projection date.

The advantages of the extrapolation approach are that it is easily undertaken and requires little expertise, other than discernment when choosing among various functions that have been fitted to the data. Although basically mechanical, the process of extrapolation is ultimately reliant on the analyst's judgment. A good understanding of the likely behaviour of the variable under examination can lead to a judicious choice of a function that may not produce the best fit with the observations as measured by the MAPE.

The major disadvantage of the extrapolation approach is that, judgment aside, it is atheoretic; that is, it does not incorporate behavioural considerations into the projection process. Second, when used to project population levels, it yields no detail with regard to the composition of the population.

Mathematical extrapolation is suitable for use for any geographical region smaller than a province or state. Because of its inability to incorporate structural change in the behaviour of the variable under consideration, it is best applied to short-range projections, say, in the 5-10 year range.

Comparative Methods

The comparative methods approach to demographic projection focuses on the relation of the local population to that of another area, generally a parent population. The two principal classes of comparative methods are the ratio and difference methods. Projections made by means of ratio methods are based on particular assumptions regarding the relationship between the sizes of the local and parent populations. Difference methods, which appear to be less frequently applied, are based on assumptions regarding the differential between the growth rates of the two populations.

The advantages of comparative methods are much the same as those of mathematical extrapolation. Comparative methods are easily applied and require little technical expertise. Additionally, it may be argued that in particular circumstances comparative methods incorporate into the process of projecting the local population the greater resources at the disposal of analysts undertaking projections of a larger, parent population. The disadvantage is that they also incorporate into the local projection process the errors and misjudgments of these same analysts. Further, in empirical tests to date, comparative methods do not produce reliably superior accuracy, even when errors in predicting the parent population are discounted.

Overall, comparative methods have little to recommend them over mathematical extrapolation for projecting population levels. They are likely better suited to the projection of birth and death rates. Age-specific birth rates may vary between the local and parent populations because of differences, for example, in degrees of urbanization. Death rates may vary because of differences in occupational patterns or environmental conditions. Comparative methods are best applied in situations in which there is confidence in both the stability of the demographic relationship between the local and parent areas and in the prediction capabilities of those responsible for the projection of the parent area variable.

Like the mathematical extrapolation approach, the comparative methods approach will not yield information regarding the composition of the population and is most appropriately applied for short-range projections. The approach will not foresee structural changes in the future path to be traced by population change unless the scope for these changes is incorporated in the process by which the parent population is projected or is introduced at the local level through judgment.

The Cohort-Survival Model

The cohort-survival approach to projection differs qualitatively from the former two approaches in that it disaggregates the population into cohorts (i.e., population segments of uniform age and sex). Projections are made on the basis of assumptions regarding cohort birth and survival rates over the projection period.

The significant advantage of the cohort-survival approach is the detail it yields with regard to the projected population. A disadvantage of the model is that it requires substantially more input data than do the simpler extrapolation and comparison approaches. It is also generally argued that the model requires substantially greater expertise for application, but this argument is somewhat weakened by the ease with which this expertise can be acquired. In its basic form as described in Chapter 5, the model focuses on the natural change of the population. The migration component of the projected population must be dealt with independently. The cohort-survival approach may thus be combined with other approaches considered in the text. The latter may be used to project cohort migration as well as birth and survival rates.

The cohort-survival model is likely most appropriately applied at or above the level of the county or large municipality and over longer periods relative to the extrapolation and comparison approaches. Its popularity of application is attributable primarily to the detail that it yields, and, when such detail is needed, it is generally the model of choice over economic-demographic models constructed through regression analysis.

Migration Models

Migration is commonly the most volatile component of population change and thus the most difficult to predict. As population registers are not kept in North America, time-series data on regions and small areas are usually not available. Without such data, mathematical extrapolation of migration flows is not feasible. Attempts to create a series of past observations can be undertaken by means of administrative records such as those pertaining to hydro connections and property tax billings. A major limitation of this method, however, is the extensive amount of data required and the level of expertise needed to properly analyze it.

Alternatively, past migration flows over an intercensal period can be estimated by indirect methods that focus on estimating the natural change in population, thus determining net migration as a residual. The vital statistics methods and the cohort-survival method are the two principal approaches to such estimation. Unless deaths are recorded by age in the collection of vital statistics data, the cohort-survival method possesses the significant comparative advantage of yielding age- and sex-specific migration estimates.

Regression models in which migration is the dependent variable constitute the principal alternative to mathematical extrapolation for projecting gross or net migration flows. The dominant focus of current research, these models are appealing in that they incorporate any number of explanatory variables. Of all the approaches considered, however, they are by far the most demanding in terms of expertise, data, and time for construction.

Summary

In sum, there is no one approach to projection that is superior to all others in every set of circumstances. The choice among the techniques will depend on the desired level of detail, available resources (including expertise), the length of the projection period, and the ends to which the projections are to be put. It is also fair to say that, unlike methods of estimation, there is no convincing evidence to date to support the proposition that more sophisticated methods of projections yield consistently better results than do simpler methods. Further, one can conclude from the evidence currently available that for regions and small areas the accuracy of prediction will be higher the larger the population to be predicted, the shorter the prediction period, and the smaller the relative significance of the migration component.

Addendum: Qualities of a Good Demographic Analyst

An enormous proportion of our daily efforts are devoted to attempts to predict future events. The focus of these efforts ranges from matters at the individual level (such as next weekend's weather, questions that may appear on the next exam, and who will wear what to the party tomorrow night) to elements at the more macro level (such as interest rates, stock prices, and voting behaviour). Fully satisfactory accuracy of predictions is rarely achieved. As Mark Twain observed some time ago, "the art of prophecy is very difficult—especially with respect to the future." While it is indeed difficult to see clearly into the future, we do know that future events are in some ways intrinsically linked to the past. Fortunately, this is particularly the case with regard to demographic matters. The task of predicting future demographic events is daunting but not infeasible.

For the analyst making demographic forecasts and projections that will later be compared with actual counts, there are perhaps three highly desirable qualities to possess.[2]   First, it is crucial to have a thorough understanding of the past behaviour of the demographic variable of concern and its principal underlying determinants; second, it is advantageous to have a sound knowledge of the present, to know which of the past trends are now dominant, and to have current information on these trends; and third, in light of the inherent difficulty of dealing with the future, it is critical to maintain a healthy sense of humour.

In accordance with this third requirement, a professional planner of my acquaintance has related to me three principles of procedure based on his years of experience in preparing municipal population projections and forecasts. First, whenever possible, use someone else's work; second, if you must make your own predictions, make several and do so frequently; and third, be farsighted—attempt to arrange your vacation schedule so that you will be out of town when municipal council considers your current predictions and past achievements.

It is hoped that the present text contributes to the reduction of the need for such farsightedness.

Appendix A

Linear Regression

A prime purpose of linear regression is to predict the values of a dependent variable, given the values of one or more independent, explanatory variables. Throughout the analysis it is assumed that a linear relationship exists between the dependent and independent variables. If only one independent variable is considered, the analysis is referred to as "simple" linear regression; if two or more independent variables are employed, the analysis is known as "multiple" regression.

Simple Linear Regression

If values of the dependent variable y vary linearly with values of the independent variable x, we may express the relationship between the two variables mathematically as

$$y = a + bx \qquad (A.1)$$

On a graph of the observations of the values of the two variables, the task of simple linear regression is to "fit" a line to the data or observation points in such a manner that the sum of the squares of the deviations of the observation points from that line is a minimum. For this reason linear regression is termed a "least squares" method of curve fitting.

To illustrate, in each of the two cases shown below, a line has been fitted to the three points on the graph (see Figure 22). Each point on the graph represents an observation of x and of the associated value of y. In case (a) the line drawn through the observations of x and y perfectly fits the data. The sum of the deviations of the data points from the line is zero. In case (b) the sum of the deviations (+1, -2, +1) is also zero, but the line is clearly not as good a fit to the data as is the line in case (a). To avoid the off-setting effects of plus and minus deviations, the deviations are squared prior to their summation. The process of squaring eliminates the significance of the positive and negative signs of the deviations; it also assigns proportionately greater weights to those data points which lie furthest from the line.

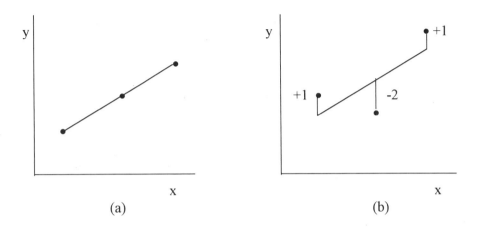

Figure 22. Regression lines: case (a) and case (b)

Illustrative Example: Simple Linear Regression

Suppose we have ten pairs of observations of x and y as shown below:

Observation :	1	2	3	4	5	6	7	8	9	10
y :	13	20	13	25	6	8	31	10	39	20
x :	10	11	5	9	2	3	13	6	12	8

A plot of the ten observations reveals a definite positive relationship between the two variables x and y (see Figure 23). Assuming values of y to vary with values of x, we may presume a linear relationship between the two variables as represented by equation (A.1).

The task of simple linear regression is to construct estimates $\hat{a}$ and $\hat{b}$ of the parameters a and b in equation (A.1) in order to obtain an estimate $\hat{y}$ of y,[1] where

$$\hat{y} = \hat{a} + \hat{b}x \qquad (A.2)$$

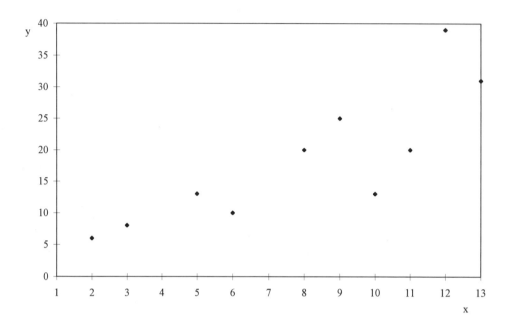

Figure 23. Observations of x and y

These estimates can be calculated as follows:[2]

$$\hat{b} = \frac{nxy - xy}{nx^2 - (x)^2} \tag{A.3}$$

$$\hat{a} = \frac{y - \hat{b}x}{n} \tag{A.4}$$

The parameters $\hat{a}$ and $\hat{b}$ can be calculated by means of a pocket/desk calculator, the regression programs of currently popular software (e.g., SPSS [Statistical Package for the Social Science], SAS [Statistical Analysis System], BMDP [Bio-MeDical computer Program]) or any number of electronic spreadsheets such as Lotus 1-2-3, Excel, or Quattro Pro. The results produced by the regression program in Lotus are as follows:

Regression Output:

Constant   -0.22343
Std Err of Y Est   6.107868
R Squared   0.708119
No. of Observations   10
Degrees of Freedom   8

X Coefficients(s)   2.370054
Std Error of Coeff.   0.537976

It can be seen from the above regression results that $\hat{a}$ = -0.223 and $\hat{b}$ = 2.370. Substituting these values into our regression equation (A.2), $\hat{y} = -0.223 + 2.370x$. For any value of x, we may now use this equation to generate a corresponding estimate $\hat{y}$ of y. For example, if in period 11 the value of x is assumed or forecast to be 12, $\hat{y}$ is then calculated to be -0.223 + 2.370(12) = 28.22.

Each of the items in our regression output is now considered in more detail below.

Constant

The constant, -0.223, is the y-intercept of the regression equation. While it is generally not the focus of the regression analyst's attention, it is necessary for calculating the projected value of y, given a new value of x, as was seen in the above calculation of $\hat{y}$ = 28.22 when x = 12.

Standard Error of Y Estimate

The standard error of estimate s_e is a measure of the average estimation error.

$$s_e = \sqrt{\frac{(y - \hat{y})^2}{n - 2}} \qquad (A.5)$$

The statistic is similar in concept to the standard deviation, which is a measure of the dispersion of a set of numbers about their average. (The standard deviation is defined as $\sqrt{(y - \bar{y})^2/(n - 1)}$ where $\bar{y}$ is the mean of n observations of y.) The standard error s_e is a measure of the dispersion of the observations about the regression line. In our example, the s_e is 6.108.[3] The greater the magnitude of s_e, the less reliable is the estimate $\hat{y}$ of y.[4]

R Squared

Once the regression line has been constructed, the question may be asked: how well does it fit the data? In other words, to what extent are values of the dependent variable correlated with values of the independent variable? An informal answer to this question can be gained from looking at the "scatterplot" of the values of the dependent and independent variables. The closer the points are clustered about the regression line, the better the line fits the data. A more formal approach to determining the strength of association between the two variables is to calculate the coefficient of determination, commonly called the "R squared."

The coefficient of determination represents the per cent of variance of the dependent variable that is attributable to variation in the independent variable. It is calculated as

$$R^2 = \frac{(\hat{y} - \bar{y})^2}{(y - \bar{y})^2} \tag{A.6}$$

For our example, the coefficient of determination, or "R-squared", is .708, which means that approximately 71% of the variation in y is explained by variation in x. Clearly, the higher the coefficient of determination, the higher is the explanatory power of the regression model.

It must be emphasized, however, that the coefficient of determination is a measure of association or correlation, and that a high degree of *correlation* does not necessarily imply *causality*. The basis for causality lies in theory rather than in regression analysis. If theoretical reasoning leads us to believe that y is dependent on x, regression analysis can *disprove* the theory: if there is no statistically acceptable correlation between y and x, there is obviously no causal relationship. On the other hand, however, regression analysis cannot *prove* the theory; it can only verify or support it. A high degree of correlation may exist between y and x when there is no causal relationship at all. The correlation may be entirely spurious or it may exist because both variables are causally linked to a second independent variable, which is not included in the equation. In still other cases, it is possible that the independent variable is defined so broadly that it contains an amalgam of several factors, each of which is linked in varying degrees to the dependent variable.

Number of Observations and Degrees of Freedom

In regression analysis the number of degrees of freedom is equal to the number of observations minus the number of parameters to be estimated from the observations. The fewer the number of parameters, or constants, to be inferred, the greater the freedom to draw inferences from the data. In simple linear regression, the number of parameters to be estimated is two: a and b. In our numerical example consisting of ten observations, there are thus eight (10 - 2) degrees of freedom.

X Coefficient

The x coefficient refers to the coefficient $\hat{b}$ in equation (A.2) and reveals the expected change in the dependent variable per unit change in the independent variable. Thus, in our example, the x coefficient value of 2.370 means that for every unit increase (decrease) in x, the regression equation leads us to expect an increase (decrease) of 2.370 units in y.

Standard Errors of the Coefficients

Analysis of the standard errors of the regression coefficient estimates is a means by which we can assess the reliability of these estimates. Of the two coefficients, the analyst's interest is generally more focused on $\hat{b}$ than on $\hat{a}$. The $\hat{b}$ coefficient tells us how much change will result in the dependent variable y, the variable whose value we are attempting to project, per unit change in the independent variable x. The y-intercept, $\hat{a}$, is frequently of no meaning in the context of the problem under study. Hence our concern is generally with the $\hat{b}$ coefficient.

The standard error, $s_{\hat{b}}$, for the $\hat{b}$ coefficient is constructed as

$$s_{\hat{b}} = \sqrt{\frac{(y_i - \hat{y}_i)^2}{(n-2)(x_i - \bar{x})^2}} \qquad (A.7)$$

The measure $s_{\hat{b}}$ is an estimate of the dispersion that would occur among the slope coefficients (i.e., the $\hat{b}$ coefficients) of many samples, were the samples to be drawn randomly from the same population. For our hypothetical data, $s_{\hat{b}}$ is calculated from equation (A.7) to be 0.538.

From the standard error of the coefficient we may construct a measure called the "t statistic"

$$t = \frac{\hat{b} - b}{s_{\hat{b}}} \qquad (A.8)$$

which follows Student's t distribution with n - 2 degrees of freedom. The t statistic measures the number of standard errors that $\hat{b}$ differs from b. It may be employed to test the hypothesis that b is zero, i.e., that y does *not* depend on x. As the initial step, a level of significance is designated for the test. Reference is then made to a t distribution table, a portion of which is shown in Table 6 with designated levels of significance and degrees of freedom.

In our example there are eight degrees of freedom (ten observations - two estimated parameters, a and b). A significance level of 5% has been arbitrarily chosen. From Table 6 the range of t values for which the hypothesis that b equals zero is true is -2.306 to +2.306. In other words, if b is in fact zero, then there is a 95% probability that our t value will fall within the range of -2.306 to +2.306.

Table 6. A selected portion of the t distribution

Significance level :	1%	2%	5%	10%
Degrees of freedom :				
10	3.169	2.764	2.228	1.812
9	3.250	2.821	2.262	1.833
8	3.355	2.896	2.306	1.860
7	3.499	2.998	2.365	1.860
6	3.707	3.143	2.447	1.943
5	4.032	3.365	2.571	2.015

Source: R.A. Fisher. 1970. *Statistical Methods for Research Workers*. University of Adelaide

The next step is to substitute zero for b in equation (A.8). From our data, t = (2.370 - 0) / 0.538 = 4.405, which is outside the range. Hence, we reject the null hypothesis that b is zero and state that $\hat{b}$ is significant (i.e., significantly different from zero) at the 5% level.[5]

When reporting regression equations, it is customary to report the standard errors of the coefficients as well. In our case the regression equation might be stated as

$$\hat{y} = -0.223 + 2.370x \qquad \text{(A.9)}$$

$$(0.538)$$

At the standard 5% level of significance, the t statistic is approximately 2. (For example, with a sample size of 25 the t statistic is 2.060; its value approaches 1.960 as the sample size approaches infinity.) Thus if one is testing to determine if a coefficient b is significantly different from zero at this level, there is a 95% chance that our estimate $\hat{b}$ will fall in the range -2 to +2. Since from equation (A.8) with b = 0, the t variable is calculated as $t_b = \hat{b}/s_b$, we can readily conclude that if $|\hat{b}/s_b| > 2$, then $\hat{b}$ is significant at the 5% level. In our illustrative regression of equation (A.2), we must be a bit more precise with our t test, since we have only ten observations. From Table 6 at the 5% level of significance and ten observations (eight degrees of freedom), the value of the t statistic is 2.306. It can thus be seen that the $\hat{b}$ coefficient is significant at the 5% level, since $t_b = 2.370/0.538 = 4.405$, which substantially exceeds 2.306.

Multiple Linear Regression

Multiple linear regression is merely an extension of simple linear regression to cases of two or more explanatory variables. For the case of two independent variables x_1 and x_2, a graph of y vs. x_1 and x_2 may be constructed. Each point in the three-dimensional space defined by the graph represents an observation of the associated values of the three variables. The task of multiple regression in this case parallels that of simple regression. As it was the objective of the latter to construct a *line* from which the sum of squared deviations of the observations of the dependent variable is a minimum, it is the aim of multiple regression to construct a *plane* about which the sum of the squared deviations of observations is minimized.

The linear equation of multiple regression for the general case of n explanatory variables is

$$y = a + b_1x_1 + b_2x_2 + \cdots + b_nx_n \qquad (A.10)$$

The b coefficients are referred to as the "beta" or partial regression coefficients. The coefficient b_i is interpreted as the change in y that results from a change in x_i when the values of the $n - 1$ remaining independent variables are held constant.

With multiple linear regression, we may construct estimates $\hat{b}_i$ of the coefficients b_i in equation (A.10) in order to determine an estimate $\hat{y}$ of y where

$$\hat{y} = \hat{a} + \hat{b}_1x_1 + \hat{b}_2x_2 + ... + \hat{b}_nx_n \qquad (A.11)$$

Illustrative Example: Multiple Linear Regression

As an illustration of multiple regression analysis, let us suppose that in addition to our previous ten bivariate observations, we have ten associated observations of a second independent variable, x_2, upon which, in theory, the value of y also depends. The value of x_2, as well as the previous observations of y and x (now labelled x_1), are shown below.

Observation :	1	2	3	4	5	6	7	8	9	10
y :	13	20	13	25	6	8	31	10	39	20
x_1 :	10	11	5	9	2	3	13	6	12	8
x_2 :	55	114	51	106	49	58	129	41	137	121

Estimates $\hat{b}_1$ and $\hat{b}_2$ may be constructed by regressing y against x_1 and x_2. The results produced by the regression program in Lotus 1-2-3 are as follows:

Regression Output:

Constant		-4.32464
Std Err of Y Est		4.524884
R Squared		0.859831
No. of Observations		10
Degrees of Freedom		7
X Coefficient(s)	1.003428	0.173026
Std Error of Coeff.	0.636669	0.062860

Briefly, it can be seen from the above results that our regression equation is

$$y = -4.325 + 1.003x_1 + 0.173x_2 \qquad (A.12)$$

Equation (A.12) reveals that a unit change in x_1 will produce an estimated change in y of 1.003 units, assuming no change in x_2. Likewise, for every unit change in x_2, with x_1 held constant, there is an estimated change in y of 0.173 units.

Each of the regression statistics shown above is now considered in more detail.

Constant

As in the case of simple or bivariate regression analysis, the constant is the y-intercept of the regression function. It is necessary for the determination of the estimate $\hat{y}$ of the dependent variable y from equation (A.11), given values for the independent variables x_1 and x_2.

Standard Error of Y Estimate

The standard error s_e is interpreted in the same manner as in simple, bivariate linear regression. It is calculated by equation (A.5).

R Squared

Parallel to bivariate regression, the explanatory power of the multiple regression equation is indicated by R^2, which in the case of multiple regression is termed the coefficient of multiple determination. The R^2 coefficient is again defined by equation (A.6) and reveals the amount of variation in the dependent variable y explained by variations in the independent variables. From the statistics yielded by the computer spreadsheet, it can be seen that 86% of the variation in y is explained by changes in x_1 and x_2. Assuming a valid theoretical basis for adding x_2 to our regression model, the explanatory power of the model has been enhanced, as is evidenced by the increase in the value of R^2 from its previous value of 71%.

Number of Observations and Degrees of Freedom

In the numerical example, there are ten observations. As stated above in the numerical illustration for simple regression analysis, the degrees of freedom are equal to the number of observations minus the number of parameters to be estimated. Since there are three parameters (y, x_1, and x_2) to be estimated in our current example, the degrees of freedom are seven (10 - 3).

X Coefficients

The X coefficients are the $\hat{b}_i$ of equation (A.11). The coefficient for our independent variable x_1 from the regression output is 1.003. This means that for every unit increase (decrease) in x_1, we can expect y to increase (decrease) by 1.003 units, assuming no change in the value of x_2. Similarly, we can expect an increase (decrease) of 0.173 units in y for every unit increase (decrease) in x_2, assuming an unchanged x_1.

Standard Errors of the Coefficients

From our regression output, the standard errors of the estimates of b_1 and b_2 are seen to be 0.637 and 0.063, respectively. As is the case with simple linear regression, we may use the t statistic to test the significance of each of our regression coefficients.

Summary

Simple linear regression is a statistical technique for empirically estimating the parameters (i.e., the constant and slope coefficient) of a linear relationship between two variables, given pairs of observations of the variables. Multiple linear regression is an extension of simple linear regression to cases of two or more independent variables. In addition to producing estimates of the parameters of a presumed linear relationship between a dependent and one or more independent variables, the analysis produces a number of statistics that are useful in making judgments about the confidence one can place in the regression's estimates.

Regression analysis can be readily undertaken on a calculator containing specialized statistical functions. Alternatively, the analysis can be performed on a computer, using statistics-oriented software or any one of several commonly employed spreadsheet programs.

Appendix B

Logarithms

In the mathematical expressions x^2 and x^5, the powers to which the variable x is raised are the constants 2 and 5, respectively. A general expression of a variable y that is dependent on another variable x raised to a power is

$$y = ax^b \qquad \text{(B.1)}$$

where a and b are constants. Equation (B.1) is known as a *power function*. A graph of the function is shown in Figure 24.

Unfortunately, linear regression is not directly applicable in determining the values of the constants a and b in the above equation, since the relationship between y and x is non-linear. As will be demonstrated below, however, non-linear relationships can be transformed into linear ones through the use of logarithms. Once the transformation is made, linear regression can then be employed to estimate the values of unknown parameters in the original non-linear equation.

What Is a Logarithm?

In the equation (B.2) below, the result of raising the base a to the exponent b is c.

$$a^b = c \qquad \text{(B.2)}$$

The relationship between the constants or parameters a, b, and c in equation (B.2) can also be expressed in terms of a logarithm:

$$log_a c = b \qquad \text{(B.3)}$$

The logarithm of a particular number is defined as the power to which a fixed number, the base, must be raised to produce the number. From equation (B.3), the logarithm of c to the base a is b.

92

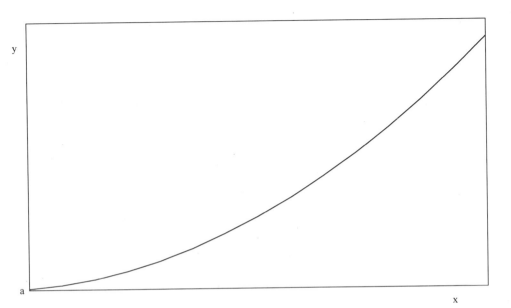

Figure 24. The power function

Exponential expression	*Logarithmic expression*
$2^3 = 8$	$log_2 8 = 3$
$5^2 = 25$	$log_5 25 = 2$
$4^{-2} = 1/16$	$log_4(1/16) = -2$

Note that in the above examples, the logarithms are of positive numbers. Every positive number has a unique logarithm. For zero and negative numbers, however, logarithms are undefined.

The base of a logarithm is not restricted to a particular number. In practice, however, one of two numbers is generally adopted as the logarithmic base: 10 and e. The latter is a number of the same nature as π and equals 2.71828. (For a discussion of the "origin" of e, see Hummelbrunner [1982: 207–09].) If the base 10 is used, the logarithm is known as a "common logarithm" and is customarily written as "log" without specifically expressing the base as 10. For example:

$$log\,100 = 2 \quad (= log_{10}100)$$
$$log\,10 = 1 \quad (= log_{10}10)$$
$$log\,1 = 0 \quad (= log_{10}1)$$
$$log\,0.1 = -1 \quad (= log_{10}0.1)$$
$$log\,0.01 = -2 \quad (= log_{10}0.01)$$

Logarithms to the base e are termed "natural" logarithms and are written as "ln" without specifically expressing the base as e. For example:

$$ln\,100 = 4.605 \quad (= ln_e 100)$$
$$ln\,10 = 2.303 \quad (= ln_e 10)$$
$$ln\,1 = 0 \quad (= ln_e 1)$$
$$ln\,0.1 = -2.303 \quad (= ln_e 0.1)$$
$$ln\,0.01 = -4.605 \quad (= ln_e 0.01$$

The Three Basic Rules of Logarithms

The rules listed below are stated in terms of natural logarithms but hold as well for common logarithms.

1. The logarithm of a product of two (or more) numbers is the sum of the logarithms of the numbers.

$$ln(ab) = ln\ a + ln\ b \quad (a, b > 0) \tag{B.4}$$

For example, $ln(100\ x\ 10) = ln\,100 + ln\,10$. The natural logarithm for the number 100 (and other positive numbers) can readily be determined by any one of three different means: consulting a published table of natural logarithms, manipulating a calculator capable of computing natural logarithms, or using a computer.

2. The logarithm of the quotient of two numbers is equal to the logarithm of the numerator minus the logarithm of the denominator.

$$ln(a/b) = ln\ a - ln\ b \quad (a, b > 0) \tag{B.5}$$

For example, $ln(10/100) = ln\,10 - ln\,100$.

3. The logarithm of a number raised to a power is the product of the power and the logarithm of the number.

$$ln(a^b) = b\ ln\ a \quad (a > 0) \tag{B.6}$$

For example, $ln\,100^{10} = 10\ ln\,100$.

To see how logarithms can help us to perform certain mathematical operations, let us look at three illustrations. First, let us solve equation (B.7), which involves simple multiplication, for the value of y.

$$y = (5)(2) \tag{B.7}$$

The value of y in the equation is obviously ten, but let us obtain that result by means of logarithms. The first step is to use rule 1 to find the logarithm of y.

$$ln\ y = ln5 + ln2 = 1.609 + 0.693 = 2.303 \qquad \text{(B.8)}$$

Once the logarithm of y has been determined, the value of y can be found by calculating the "anti-logarithm," the opposite of the logarithm. For example, the antilogarithm (written as "antiln") of the number 2.303 is 10 and is calculated by raising e to the power of 2.303.

$$y = antiln(ln\ y) = antiln(2.303) = 10 \qquad \text{(B.9)}$$

As is the case with computing logarithms, antilogarithms are found by means of logarithmic tables, by calculators, or by use of a computer.

Let us consider a second illustration in which the value of y is not obvious.

$$y = (10)(5^{2.6})(6^{0.2}) \qquad \text{(B.10)}$$

To solve for y in equation (B.10), logarithm rules 1 and 3 are employed.

$$ln\ y = ln10 + 2.6(ln5) + 0.2(ln6) \qquad \text{(B.11)}$$

$$y = antiln(ln10 + 2.6(ln5) + 0.2(ln6) = antiln(6.845) = 939.62 \qquad \text{(B.12)}$$

As a final illustration, let us solve for y in equation (B.13).

$$y = 12 + 4.2^{3.1}/6.5 \qquad \text{(B.13)}$$

In this case, rules 2 and 3 are used. The logarithm of y is constructed in two steps. Since we have no rule for determining the logarithm of a sum, the first step is to find the value of the second expression on the right-hand side of the equation.

$$antiln[3.1(ln4.2) - ln6.5] = antiln[3.1(1.435) - 1.872] = 13.16 \qquad \text{(B.14)}$$

The value of y may now be calculated via simple addition as $y = 12 + 13.16 = 25.16$.

Logarithms and Linear Transformations

In making demographic projections, the analyst is often faced with the task of estimating the parameters of a non-linear mathematical function. Since linear regression yields estimates of the parameters of a linear function, it is applicable only if the non-linear function can be transformed into an equivalent linear expression. Logarithms make such transformations possible. To illustrate, let's draw upon what we have learned about logarithms and about linear regression for the purpose of estimating the parameters of a non-linear relationship, the power function of equation (B.1). The first step in the estimation of the parameters a and b is to use logarithms to transform the non-linear relationship between the variables y and x to a linear one.

$$ln\ y = ln\ a + b\ ln\ x \qquad (B.15)$$

Equation (B.15) can be rewritten as

$$y' = a' + bx' \qquad (B.16)$$

where $y' = ln\ y$, $a' = ln\ a$, and $x' = ln\ x$. We may now write the corresponding regression equation,

$$\hat{y}' = \hat{a}' + \hat{b}x' \qquad (B.17)$$

where $\hat{a}'$ and $\hat{b}$ are the regression estimates of a' and b, respectively. Thus,

$$\hat{y} = antiln(\hat{a}' + \hat{b}x') \qquad (B.18)$$

Once values for $\hat{a}'$ and $\hat{b}$ have been determined, the estimate of y for any value of x may be calculated via equation (B.18).

To illustrate, suppose we set the parameters of equation (B.1) at $a = 2, b = 3$. The associated values of y at selected values of x are thus as shown below:

$$x:\quad 1 \quad 2 \quad 3 \quad 4 \quad 5$$
$$y:\quad 2 \quad 16 \quad 54 \quad 128 \quad 250$$

Although the value of y in period six is easily determined in this simple example to be 432, let us apply linear regression to the logarithmic transformation of the power function of equation (B.1) to obtain this result. As a first step, we wish to construct estimates $\hat{a}'$ and $\hat{b}$ in equation (B.18), which shows a linear relationship between y' and x', that is, between $ln\ y$ and $ln\ x$. Using a regression program contained in a computer spreadsheet or a pre-programmed calculator, we calculate the logarithms of the observations of y and x shown above and then regress $ln\ y$ against $ln\ x$. The resulting parameter estimates are $\hat{a}' = 0.6931$ and $\hat{b} = 3$. Finding the natural logarithm of 6 to be 1.7918, we may now project y to period 6 as

$$\hat{y}_6 = antiln[0.6931 + 3(1.7918)] = 432 \qquad (B.19)$$

Summary

The logarithm of a number is the power to which a fixed base must be raised in order to produce the number. In practice, two logarithmic bases are used: ten and *e*. Common logarithms are those to the base ten, while natural logarithms are to the base *e*. Logarithms are frequently used in demographic projections based on extrapolation of mathematical functions because they permit the transformation of non-linear functions into equivalent linear forms. Knowledge of the three basic rules of logarithms is generally sufficient to perform such transformations. Once a linear relationship has been specified between a dependent and one or more independent variables, projections of future values of the dependent variable may be generated through the application of linear regression.

Notes

Chapter 1: Introduction

1 In a survey of businesses in metropolitan Vancouver, a cross-section of business owners and managers were asked what current and historic data and what kinds of projections they would need in making decisions to change their scale of operations or to relocate. In both categories, information regarding population topped the list of replies, with approximately two-thirds of the respondents identifying the need for such data. See Development Services Department, Greater Vancouver Regional District, *Economic Development Issues: Results of a Questionnaire Survey* (Vancouver 1984).

2 Labour force projections are generally derived by first projecting population by age and sex cohorts and then multiplying each projected cohort by the appropriate labour force participation rate. See, for example, J.M. Sehgal, *An Introduction to Techniques of Population and Labour Force Projections* (Geneva: International Labour Office 1986).

3 Given that some degree of divergence between projected and actual outcomes is generally inevitable, the bias toward projections that are too low or too high can vary with the use to which the projections are put. For example, if one is projecting population for the purpose of deciding the capacity of sewer lines, it is likely desirable to project on the high side. Once the sewer lines are laid, the cost of replacing them with lines of greater diameter can be prohibitive. Users of demographic projections for the purpose of predicting retail sales levels, however, may prefer a bias toward underestimation. A volume of sales somewhat greater than expected can likely be handled by existing sales staff and floor space; overestimation of the population may cause unnecessary expenditures on staff or capital expansion.

4 For a journalistic sketch of a range of Canadian socioeconomic phenomena affected by demographics, see D. Stoffman, "Completely Predictable People," *Report on Business Magazine* (November 1990):78-84.

5 A.M. Isserman and P.S. Fisher, "Population Forecasting and Local Economic Planning: The Limits of Community Control over Uncertainty," *Population Research and Policy Review* 3

(1984):27-50. A critical discussion of the issues raised in the paper can be found in E.W. Moen, "Population Forecasting and Planning: Some Philosophical Issues," *Population Research and Policy Review* 3 (1984):51-60.

6 A similar proactive approach is recommended by Breheny and Roberts, who suggest that planners should construct projections or forecasts of "desirable futures" detailing what needs to occur to effect such futures. See M.J. Breheny and A.J. Roberts, "Forecasting Methodologies in Strategic Planning: A Review," *Papers of the Regional Science Association* 44 (1980):75-90.

7 E.W. Moen, "Voodoo Forecasting: Technical, Political and Ethical Issues Regarding the Projection of Local Population Growth, *Population Research and Policy Review* 3 (1984):180.

8 See, for example, H. Hightower, "Population Studies," ed. W. Goodman and E. Freund, *Principles and Practice of Urban Planning* (Washington, DC: International City Managers' Association 1968); N. Keyfitz, "On Future Population," *Journal of the American Statistical Association* 67 (1972):347-63); D. Pittenger, *Projecting State and Local Populations* (Cambridge, MA: Ballinger 1976); R. Irwin, *Guide for Local Area Population Projections*, Technical Paper No. 39 (Washington, DC: U.S. Bureau of the Census 1977).

9 Not all population analysts, however, are inclined to such forgiveness. For example, D.B. Pittenger, "Some Problems in Forecasting Population for Government Planning Purposes," *The American Statistician* 34 (1980):135-39, argues that extrapolation devoid of judgment is generally justifiable only when the analyst is ignorant of the conditions that influenced growth, perceives demonstrably strong historical and continued inertia, or is forecasting for a very short (2-3 year) period of time.

10 A.M. Isserman and P.S. Fisher, "Population Forecasting and Local Economic Planning: The Limits on Community Control over Uncertainty," *Population and Policy Review* 3 (1984):27-50.

11 D. Pittenger, "Some Problems in Forecasting," 3. For a broader definition of population estimates, see H.S. Shryock and J.S. Siegel, *The Methods and Materials of Demography* (Washington: U.S. Bureau of the Census 1973), 725.

12 The household unit method of population estimation divides the population into two groups: private households and group quarters. The former, which generally accounts for more than 90 per cent of the population, consists of all persons who live in household units such as single family dwellings, duplexes, apartments, condominiums, and townhouses. Persons in group quarters consist of those who have been institutionalized (e.g., residents of nursing homes and penal and mental institutions) and persons who reside in group facilities such as college dormitories and military barracks. Population is thus the number of households multiplied by the average number of persons per household plus the group-quarters population. That is, population P_t at time t can be expressed as

$$P_t = H_t HS_t + GQ_t$$

where H_t = the number of households,
HS_t = the average household size, and
GQ_t = the group-quarters population.

For a discussion of this approach to population, see S.K. Smith and B.B. Lewis, "Accuracy of the Housing Unit Method in Preparing Population Estimates for Cities," *Demography* 5 (1980):475-84; D.E. Starsinic and M. Zitter, "Some New Techniques for Applying the Housing

Unit Method of Local Population Estimation," *Demography* 17 (1968):323-39. For other methods of postcensal population estimation, see J.C. Raymondo, *Population Estimation and Projection* (New York: Quorum Books 1992), 123-60.

Chapter 2: Mathematical Extrapolation I

1 If for each value of the variable *x* there is only one corresponding value *y*, *y* is said to be a *function* of *x*. Mathematical extrapolation can be defined as the projection of the values of a function beyond those of the observed range.

2 A more detailed discussion of each of these "standard" or commonly employed functions can be found in A.G. Wilson and M.J. Kirby, *Mathematics for Geographers and Planners* (New York: Oxford University Press 1980).

3 The choice of the first two pairs of observations of *x* and *y* is arbitrary. From the above derivation of *b* in equation (2.5) it is readily apparent that any two successive pairs of observations of *x* and *y* will result in a slope of *b*. The slope of a straight line is thus constant throughout its length.

4 In this case a regression line was fitted to our data in such a way as to minimize the sum of the squares of the deviations to the observations from the line. It is sometimes suggested by demographic analysts that the accuracy of the projection estimate may be improved by forcing the regression line through the last observation. For example, in his empirical test of a number of mathematical functions for ten-year population projections for 1,777 townships in Illinois and Indiana, Isserman (1977) used both "line" projections (extensions of regression lines) and "point" projections (parallel shifts of the regression line so that it passes through the last observed population point). It was found that point projections were slightly more accurate on average than were line projections.

   The reasoning is that the last observation is the base from which population expands into the next period and should therefore be weighted more heavily than previous observations in the projection procedure. Assuming the rate of increase of population (i.e., the slope *b* of the regression line) to be unchanged, equation (2.6) may be rewritten to obtain a projected value for population at, say, time *t* + 1 as

   $$P_{t+1} = P_t + b$$

   Our projected population at *t* = 5 in this case is thus $P_5 = P_4 + b = 1,806 + 201.8 = 2,008$.

5 In estimating total U.S. population for five- and ten-year periods, this simple geometric projection model was found to be superior to much more complex methods. See M.A. Stoto, "The Accuracy of Population Projections," *Journal of the American Statistical Association* 78 (1983):13-20.

6 In all examples in the text using logarithms, natural rather than common logarithms are applied. See Appendix B for definitions of each.

7 Alternatively, as was the case with the linear function, one may choose to give particular weight to the last observation by forcing the regression line through this point. For the exponential curve, the relevant equation would be

   $$lnP_{t+1} = lnP_t + ln\ b$$

   The projection of our hypothetical population data to *t* = 5 would thus be P_5 = antiln(ln P_4 + ln b) = antiln(ln 2875 + .2662) = 3,752.

8 While the extrapolation techniques discussed in this chapter can be easily applied through the use of electronic spreadsheets or the construction of simple computer programs, there are a number of existing software packages specially designed for the extension of past time series. For a review of several of these time series packages that allow use of a personal computer to introduce various degrees of statistical sophistication into the projection process, see R. Cervero, "Forecasting on the PC," *American Planning Association Journal* 53 (1987):510-20.

Chapter 3: Mathematical Extrapolation II

1 For the derivation of formulas to determine c as well as a and b, given values of P_t and t, see Croxton, Cowden, and Klein (1967:262-67).
2 A major shortcoming of both the MSE and MAPE measures is their failure to yield any evidence of bias (i.e., direction of error) in the projection method being tested. For example, suppose that a particular projection method tested over several sets of data yields overestimations in 90% of the applications. The knowledge that the method generally overestimates is useful information to the analyst for at least two reasons. First, as discussed in Chapter 1, the nature of the social and economic problems that result from projections or forecasts that are too high differ in particular applications from those that are too low. Second, knowledge of the bias of a technique is useful if modifications of the technique are to be attempted in order to improve its accuracy. As an alternative to modifying the technique to diminish its bias, it may be used as either an upper or lower bound, depending on the direction of its bias. The technique may then be employed in conjunction with a second technique (which produces a bias in the opposite direction) to establish the limits which enclose the "most likely" future population.
   A second problem with the MSE and MAPE measures is that each (particularly the MSE) may be significantly affected by "outliers," uncommonly high or low values. For this reason the median squared error or the median absolute percentage error is sometimes used as complementary measures of the prediction error. See, for example, D.S. O'Neil and C.D. McIntosh, "Estimating the Age/Sex Distribution of Small Area Populations," *Survey Methodology* 11 (1985):203-10 and British Columbia, *Generalized Estimation System (GES)* (Victoria: Central Statistic Bureau, Ministry of Finance and Corporate Relations 1989).
3 Croxton, Cowden, and Klein, "Analysis of Time Services," 282-83, recommend plotting the data on a semi-logarithmic scale if the graph constructed on a simple arithmetic scale is concave upwards. For further guidance in selecting a trend type, the authors offer fourteen simple tests, several involving examination of first or second differences.

Chapter 4: Comparative Methods

1 In constructing employment projections for U.S. SMSAs, a projected share model was found to be superior overall to the simple regression, constant numeric change, and constant share models. See C.E. Cina, "An Empirical Test of Nonsophisticated Employment Projection Techniques at the SMSA Level," *Regional Science Perspectives* 8 (1978):1-11.
2 For a discussion of the application of differential weights to past observations in the calculation of a moving average, see J.E. Freund and F.J. Williams, *Elementary Business Statistics: The Modern Approach* (Englewood Cliffs, NJ: Prentice-Hall 1982), 495-501.
3 LINSH and EXPSH, shown in Table 1, are subsets of the more generally defined projected share model of equation (4.4); similarly, LINDIF is but one variant of the projected difference method of equation (4.8).

4 The error ranges shown in Table 2 were constructed by calculating for each projection the ratio of the projected to actual population. Adjusting the township projections by scaling them to ensure that the sum of the projected township populations in each county is equal to the projected county population marginally lowered the prediction error for most (but not all) of the ten methods.

5 A similar test was conducted by the author for five-year demographic projections for British Columbia municipalities. The seventy-seven municipalities selected were ones which (a) were in existence throughout the 1951-81 period; (b) experienced no significant boundary changes during this period; (c) had 1981 populations less than 150,000. Three sets of projections were made to the census years 1971, 1976, and 1981, respectively, using in each case the populations of the prior four censuses.

Of the nineteen projection methods employed, eight were extrapolations and eleven involved comparisons with a parent population. For the parent population in each of the comparison methods the known population in the target year was used rather than a projected population. Despite this favourable bias built into the comparative methods, they were generally not as accurate as were the simpler extrapolation techniques in projecting populations to known values (a finding similar to Isserman's).

6 M.R. Greenberg, D.A. Krueckeberg, and C.O. Michaelson, *Local Population and Employment Projection Techniques* (New Brunswick, NJ: Center for Urban Policy Research 1978)

Chapter 5: The Cohort-Survival Population Model

1 The cohort-survival model is frequently summarized mathematically with the use of matrix notation, which has been avoided here to maintain simplicity of exposition. Matrix representation of the cohort-survival and other demographic models can be found, for example, in A. Rogers, "Matrix Methods of Population Analysis," *Journal of the American Institute of Planners* 32:40-44; P.H. Rees and A.G. Wilson, "A Comparison of Available Models of Population Change," *Regional Studies* 9 (1975):39-61; N. Oppenheim, *Applied Models in Urban and Regional Analysis* (Englewood Cliffs, NJ: Prentice-Hall 1980), 45-67.

2 Concise discussions of various mortality and fertility rates, as well as other demographic measures can be found in A. Haupt and T.T. Kane, *Population Handbook* (Washington, DC: Population Reference Bureau 1980) and J. Saunders, *Basic Demographic Measures* (New York: University Press of America 1988). For more extensive discussions of these demographic measures, see D.J. Bogue, *Principles of Demography* (New York: Wiley 1969) and C. Newell, *Methods and Models in Demography* (London: Belhaven Press 1988).

3 Because age and sex are such obviously important influences on the crude death rate, it is common practice when comparing crude death rates between two or more populations (or between two or more time periods for a single population) to weight the observed death rates with a chosen "standard" (real or assumed) population. The advantage of a standardized death rate is that it allows for comparisons of mortality between populations with the assurance that differences in age and sex composition between the populations will be of no influence. It is to be noted, however, that comparisons of standardized death rates between populations are dependent on the population selected as the standard. For further discussion, see Bogue, *Principles of Demography*, 550-52, and Saunders, *Basic Demographic Measures*, 46-49.

4 In practice, survival rates for a cohort-survival model are calculated with "weighted" one-year, age-specific death rates derived from a life table. These weighted rates differ from the observed rates only slightly for each cohort, except the first and last (infant and

terminal age) groups. See H.S. Shryock and J.S. Siegel, *The Methods and Materials of Demography* (Washington: U.S. Bureau of the Census 1980), 424. For an elementary exposition of the construction and uses of the demographer's life table, see Saunders, *Basic Demographic Measures*, 51-62.

5 Mathematical extrapolation may also be used to project mortality rates by cause of death. The U.S. Social Security Administration, for example, has projected mortality rates by each of a number of causes since 1981. For further consideration of cause-of-death specific projections of mortality rates, and the incorporation of biomedical research into the projection process, see Olshansky, "On Forecasting Mortality," *The Milbank Quarterly* 66 (1988):482-530; K.G. Manton, "Models for Forecasting Morbidity," in *Forecasting in the Social and Natural Sciences*, eds. K.L. Land and S.H. Schneider (Boston: Reidel Publishing 1986); M. Alderson and F. Ashwood, "Projection of Mortality Rates for the Elderly," *Population Trends* 42 (1985):22-29; K.G. Manton and E. Stallard, *Recent Trends in Mortality Analysis* (San Diego: Academic Press 1984).

6 Nationally, there is a long-term downward trend for overall mortality rates. National trends are not followed by every municipality and region, however. The mortality rates for any region will be determined in large part by factors such as the principal occupations of the populace and environmental conditions. However, in the absence of knowledge of such differences, we may generally expect local age-specific death rates to follow the national pattern.

7 It is a relatively simple task on a computer spreadsheet to change the value of the lower boundary of the modified exponential function to see the impact of the change on the associated MAPE. In this case, by changing the boundary value to 1.45, MAPE can be reduced to 7,129. The ASDR for males 40-44 projected to time 20 then becomes 1.88.

8 In order to make a judgment as to whether or not a population is reproducing itself, demographers frequently make observations over time of measures which are modifications of the TFR: the gross and net reproduction rates. The gross reproduction rate is the same as the TFR, save that only female births are counted in the numerator. The net reproduction rate (NRR) differs from the gross in that female mortality is taken into account by multiplying each cohort by the probability that a female in the population will survive from birth to the age of the cohort. For a population to replace itself over time, it is generally held that the number of women in the population must be at least constant from one generation to the next, that is, that the NRR $\geq$ 1.

9 For further consideration of the projection of fertility rates, see W.R. Bell, J.F. Long, R.B. Miller, and P.A. Thompson, "Multivariate Time Series Projections of Parameterized Age-Specific Fertility Rates," research report no. 88/16, Statistical Research Division, U.S. Bureau of the Census, Washington, DC, 1988; J. de Beer, "Methods of Fertility Projections," paper presented at the International Workshop on National Population Projections in Industrialized Countries, Voorburg, the Netherlands, October 1988; and R.B. Miller, P. Thompson, W. Bell, and J.F. Long, "Forecasting Graduated Age-Specific Fertility Rates," proceedings, First Annual Research Conference, U.S. Bureau of the Census, Washington, DC, 1985, 271-87.

10 L.H. Day, *Analysing Population Trends* (New York: St. Martin's Press 1983), 232-33.

11 Although female participation and fertility rates are negatively correlated, there is some debate regarding the direction of causality. See, for example, R.M. Stolzenberg and L.J. Waite, "Age Fertility Expectations and Plans for Employment," *American Sociological Review* 42 (1977):769-82; L. Smith-Lovin and A.R. Tickamyer, "Labor Force Participation, Fertility Behavior and Sex Role Attitudes," *American Sociological Review* 43 (1978):541-56. J. Cramer, "Fertility and Female Employment: Problems of Causal Direction," American Sociological Review 45

(1980):167-90, suggests that in the short run fertility is the causal factor (women leave the workforce in the later stages of pregnancy and early motherhood), while in the long run labour force participation is the dominant factor (the economic opportunity costs of parenthood induces fewer children).

12 For further consideration of family size expectations and the projection process, see R.D. Lee, "Aiming at a Moving Target: Period Fertility and Changing Reproductive Goals," *Population Studies* 24 (1980):205-260. For an interesting perspective on the influence of family size and configuration on intellectual performance, see R.B. Zajonc, "Family Configuration and Intelligence," in *Perspectives on Population*, ed. S.W. Menard and E.W. Moen (New York: Oxford University Press 1987), 408-23. See also R.J. Herrnstein, "IQ and Falling Birth Rates," *Atlantic* 263 (1988):5.

13 Offsetting to a limited degree this narrowing of the range of child-bearing years are improvements in health technology and education that tend to promote childbearing in the later years.

14 For a critical discussion of several conventional views concerning the influence of socioeconomic factors on fertility and a consideration of the implications of the relative sizes of successive generations, see R.A. Easterlin, *Birth and Fortune* (New York: Basic Books 1980). Discussions of the value of economic theory and research to the analysis of fertility and child-raising can be found in T.W. Schultz, "The Value of Children: An Economic Perspective," *Journal of Political Economy* 81 (1973):52-53 and E.P. Schultz, "Prospects for the Demand Approach to Demographic Behavior," in *Economics of Population* (Reading, MA: Addison-Wesley 1981), 227-37. For more general discussions of demographic economics, see R. Lee, "Current Issues in Economic Demography: An Overview," in *Population: Theory and Policy*, ed. R. Schoen and D. Landman (Urbana-Champaign: University of Illinois Press 1982), 21-42; J.F. Forbes, "Population Economics: A Survey of Recent Research," *Scottish Journal of Political Economy* 30 (1983):88-96; and B.M.S. van Praag, "The Notion of Population Economics," *Journal of Population Economics* 1 (1988):5-16.

15 In a comparison of projection methods applied to U.S. state populations with no regard to their age and sex profiles, the cohort-survival model (under the assumption of a constant rate of · migration) failed to yield "definitely superior results" compared with simple methods such as constant numeric change, constant rate of growth, and elementary ratio methods. See H.R. White, "Empirical Study of the Accuracy of Selected Methods of Projecting State Populations," *Journal of American Statistical Association* 29 (1954):480-98.

16 For a discussion of a modified cohort-survival projection model designed for use on a microcomputer, see N. Levine "The Construction of a Population Analysis Program Using a Microcomputer Spreadsheet," *Journal of the American Planning Association* 51 (1985):496-510. See also N.C. Field, "Population Analysis on the Microcomputer: A System of Software Packages," *Canadian Geographer* 35 (1991):23-36.

Chapter 6: Migration Models

1 E.G. Ravenstein, "The Laws of Migration," *Journal of the Royal Statistical Society* 48 (1885):167-277; E.G. Ravenstein, "The Laws of Migration," *Journal of the Royal Statistical Society* 52 (1889):241-301. The enumeration of the laws here follows the expositions of E.S. Lee, "A Theory of Migration," *Demography* 3 (1966):47-59 and D.J. Bogue, *Principles of Demography* (New York: Wiley 1969), 755-56.

2 For an evaluation of various approaches to estimating Canadian emigration, see R.B.P. Verma

and R. Raby, "The Use of Administrative Records for Estimating Population in Canada," *Survey Methodology* 15 (1989):261-70.
3   A. Rogers, *Regional Population Projection Models* (Beverly Hills: Sage 1985).
4   The dangers of so doing are well outlined in A. Rogers, "Requiem for the New Migrant," *Geographical Analysis* 22 (1990):283-300. A more sympathetic view of research focused on net rather than gross migration can be found in D.A. Plane and P.A. Rogerson, "The Ten Commandments of Migration Research," in *Regional Science: Retrospect and Prospect*, ed. D.E. Boyce, P. Nijkamp, and D. Shafer (New York: Springer-Verlag 1991).
5   This list is reproduced from Bogue, *Principles of Demography*, 753-54.
6   See Lee, "A Theory of Migration," 47-59.
7   Alonso's multiregional model ignores personal factors to focus on three types of variables: "site" variables (characteristics of origins and destinations), "situational" variables (characteristics of a region within the system of regions), and "accessibility" variables (characteristics of a region relative to another region). W. Alonso, "A Theory of Movements," in *Human Settlement Systems* (Cambridge, MA: Ballinger 1978), 197-211. For an application of the model to interregional migration in Canada, see J. Le Dent, "Forecasting Interregional Migration: An Economic-Demographic Approach," in *Population Change and the Economy: Social Science Theories and Models* (Hingham, MA: Kluwer Academic Publishers 1986), 53-77.
8   This problem extends to international migration as well, although the problem is not as severe. Records are kept of persons from other countries who legally transfer their permanent residence to Canada. Apart form foreign service personnel and their families, a landing record is kept for each new immigrant; this record contains the city and province in which location is intended. Although there are no direct measures of emigration and the number of Canadian citizens returning from foreign residences, there are indirect ways to measure both of these flows. Statistics Canada currently publishes estimates of emigrants based on family allowance accounts transferred outside Canada and U.S. records of immigration from Canada. Estimates of returning Canadians are based on information contained on Customs and Excise form E-311. (Personal communication from Dr. Don McRae, Planning and Statistics Division, Ministry of Finance, Province of British Columbia.)
9   For an exposition of the methods used by Statistics Canada to construct annual estimates of interprovincial migration flows on the basis of tax returns and family allowance payments records, see Statistics Canada, *Population Estimation Methods, Canada*, catalogue no. 91-528E (Ottawa: Supply and Services 1987), 43-68. The quality of the data on which these estimates are based is discussed in J. Vanderkamp and E.K. Grant, "Canadian Internal Migration Statistics: Some Comparisons and Evaluations," *Canadian Journal of Regional Science* 11 (1988):9-32. A comparison of censuses, surveys, and administrative records as sources of statistical data can be found in G.J. Brackstone, "Issues in the Use of Administrative Records for Statistical Purposes," *Survey Methodology* 13 (1987):29-43.
10   An extensive discussion of the problems associated with this method can be found in D.J. Bogue, K. Hinze, and M. White, *Techniques of Estimating Net Migration* (Chicago: Community and Family Study Center, University of Chicago 1982).
11   Alternatively, the census population of year t may be projected backward to t-5 by using "reverse survival rates." An argument for employing both forward and backward projections and averaging the results is made in J.S. Siegel and C.H. Hamilton, "Some Considerations in the

Use of the Residual Method of Estimating Net Migration," *Journal of the American Statistical Association* 47 (1952):475-500.

12 For taxonomies and overviews of the literature on migration, see I. Molho, "Theories of Migration: A Review." *Scottish Journal of Political Economy* 33 (1986):396-419; M.J Greenwood, P.R. Meuser, D.A. Plane, and A.M. Schlottmann, "New Directions in Migration Research," *Annals of Regional Science* 25 (1991):273-70; and M. Cadwallader, *Migration and Residential Mobility: Macro and Micro Approaches* (Madison: University of Wisconsin Press 1992).

13 For discussions of the role of amenities in the migration process, see P.E. Graves, "A Reexamination of Migration, Economic Opportunity, and the Quality of Life," *Journal of Regional Science* 16 (1976):107-12; R.J. Cebula, "The Quality of Life and Migration: A Generalized Model," in *The Determinants of Human Migration* (Toronto: Lexington 1979); T.A. Knapp and P.E. Graves, "On the Role of Amenities in Models of Migration and Regional Development," *Journal of Regional Science* 29 (1989):71-88.

14 Because of the focus of this text on regions and small areas, no distinction has been drawn between internal and international migration in the discussion of the projection process. The contribution of international migrants to the total change population is assumed to be relatively insignificant. In cases in which this assumption does not hold, international migration should be projected as a separate component of population change because of its direct impact on the age and sex structure of the receiving region, its indirect impact through natural increase, and its influence on the region's ethnic and cultural composition (Willekens, "Demographic Forecasting," 34-35). At the more macro level the use of immigration as a tool for "stabilizing" the elderly population to the working-age population has become an issue in many countries with aging populations. For an overview of this issue, see H. Zlotnik, "The Role of International Migration in the Population Equation," in *The Changing Course of International Migration* (Paris: OECD 1993), 47-54.

15 Subnational population projections can vary substantially, depending on how migration estimates are generated. For example, see J.F. MacDonald and D.W. South, "A Comparison of Two Methods to Project Regional and State Populations for the U.S.," *Annals of Regional Science* 19 (1985):40-53, for a comparison of state and regional population projections by the U.S. Bureau of the Census and Data Resources, Inc. The former assumes that age-specific net migration to each state will continue as it had in the past. The latter handles migration implicitly by assuming that the population levels of each state (region) are a function primarily of the state's (region's) share of employment and its relative wage, each calculated on the basis of a three-year moving average.

16 On a few occasions, economic-demographic models have been constructed on the basis of regional economic input-output models. See, for example, P.C. Huszar, "Projecting Regional Population with an Input-Output Model," *Growth and Change* 10 (1979):1-11; P.W.J. Batey, "Input-Output Models for Regional Demographic-Economic Analysis: Some Structural Comparisons," *Environmental and Planning* A 17 (1985):73-99.

17 Population groups that are particularly prone to migrate may be treated separately. For instance, the U.S. Bureau of the Census projects college students and military personnel independently of the general population. See S.I. Wetrogan, *Projections of the Population of States by Age, Sex, and Race: 1988 to 2010*, current population reports, series P-25, no. 1017, U.S. Bureau of the Census (Washington, DC: U.S. Government Printing Office 1988).

18 For a discussion of the economic-demographic approach, see A.M. Isserman, D.A. Plane, P.A. Rogerson, and P.M. Beaumont, "Forecasting Interstate Migration with Limited Data: A Demographic-Economic Approach," *Journal of the American Statistical Association* 80 (1985):277-85; A.M. Isserman, "Economic-Demographic Modelling with Endogenously Determined Birth and Migration Rates: Theory and Prospects," *Environment and Planning* A 17 (1985):25-45; and F.L. Leistritz, R.A. Chase, and S.H. Murdock, "Socioeconomic Impact Models: A Review of Analytical Methods and Policy Implications," in *Integrated Analysis of Regional Systems*, ed. P.W.J. Batey and M. Madden (London: Pion 1986). For a review of large-scale economic-demographic models constructed for developing countries, see R.E. Bilsborrow, "The Demographics of Macro-Economic-Demographic Models," *Population Bulletin of the United Nations* 26 (1989):39-83.

19 Ledent argues that bidirectional models are appropriate for demographic projections twenty years and beyond. See J. Ledent, "Long-Range Regional Population Forecasting: Specification of a Minimal Demoeconomic Model, with a Test for Tucson, Arizona," *Papers of the Regional Science Association* 29 (1982):37-76.

20 In his comprehensive survey of the literature pertaining to econometric forecasts of economic conditions, Armstrong found no support for either the hypothesis that complexity and accuracy are positively correlated in econometric models or that econometric models perform better than methods such as extrapolation and judgment. See J.S. Armstrong, "Forecasting with Econometric Methods: Folklore versus Fact," in *The Forecasting Accuracy of Major Time Series Methods*, ed. S. Makridakis et al. (Chicester: Wiley and Sons 1984), 19-34. Similar conclusions were reached by Ascher in a study of the use of complex models for economic and energy forecasting. See W. Ascher, "The Forecasting Potential of Complex Models," *Policy Sciences* 19 (1981):247-67, and by Raymondo, *Population Estimation and Projection* (New York: Quorum Books 1992), 197, who concludes that "the logic of the econometric approach is appealing, but the results are often not worth the effort."

21 For example, Stoto, "The Accuracy of Population Projection," 13, found that "for projections of total population size, simple projections are more accurate than complex techniques." Based on a literature review and an empirical evaluation of projections for states and counties, S.K. Smith, *Population Projections: What Do We Really Know?* (Gainesville: Bureau of Economic and Business Research, University of Florida 1984), 47, concludes that "there is no evidence that more sophisticated techniques lead to more accurate forecasts of total population than simpler extrapolation techniques." Further, support for the position of constructing simple models in all areas of forecasting is offered by the emerging field of chaos theory (the study of order without predictability beyond the immediate future). See, for example, T.J. Cartwright, "Planning and Chaos Theory," *Journal of the American Planning Association* 57 (1991):44-56.

Chapter 7: A Final Note
1 See, for example, N.R. Farnum and W.S. LaVerne, *Quantitative Forecasting Methods* (Boston: PWS-Kent Publishing 1989).

2 P.A. Morrison, *Demographic Information for Cities: A Manual for Estimating and Projecting Local Population Characteristics*, report R-618-HUD (Santa Monica, CA: RAND 1971). It has been suggested by Smith that it is also essential for the users of projections and forecasts to be imbued with the same three qualities. See S.K. Smith, *Population Projections: What Do We Really Know?* (Gainseville, FL: Bureau of Economic and Business Research 1984).

Appendix A: Linear Regression

1 If we define the difference between y and $\hat{y}$ as $\in$ for each value of x (in our case of ten observations, $\in$ takes on values $\in1$, ..., $\in10$), we may write

$$y - \hat{y} = \in \tag{A.13}$$

Substitution of (A.1) with (A.14) yields

$$y = \hat{y} + \in = \hat{a} + \hat{b}x + \in \tag{A.14}$$

For estimates $\hat{a}$ and $\hat{b}$ of the coefficients a and b and to be "best" estimates (in the sense of minimizing variance or dispersion of the $\in$'s), the residuals should be randomly distributed about the regression line. Generally, one can readily test the fulfilment of this condition by observing a plot of the residuals. (For a discussion of this and additional assumptions concerning residual errors in linear regression analysis and the implications of violations of these assumptions, see Lewis-Beck, *Applied Regression*, 26-30.)

There are two common sources for the residuals, or estimation errors, of equation (A.14). One is measurement error. For any number of reasons, inaccuracies may occur in the gathering and recording of the data. To the extent that they are not mutually off-setting, such inaccuracies will adversely affect the reliability of the predicted values of the dependent variable; that is, they will increase the magnitude of the residuals.

A second source of the difference between y and $\hat{y}$ is specification error. It may be that changes in the dependent variable are only partially attributable to changes in the independent variable that has been identified. To improve the accuracy of the estimation of the dependent variable, it may be necessary to add one or more additional independent variables to the regression equation. (Alternatively, in some cases one or more independent variables may have been inappropriately included in the regression equation and should be deleted.)

2 These so-called "normal equations" for $\hat{a}$ and $\hat{b}$ can be readily derived through elementary calculus. Since we wish to minimize the sum of the squares of the residuals, that is, $\Sigma(y_i - \hat{a} - \hat{b}x_i)^2$, we take the partial derivatives of this sum with respect to $\hat{a}$ and $\hat{b}$, set each equal to zero, and solve the two equations simultaneously. See, for example, D.A. Katz, *Econometric Theory and Application* (Englewood Cliffs, NJ: Prentice-Hall 1982), 100-1.

3 The standard error is sometimes used to construct a "confidence interval" for the estimate of the dependent variable. The confidence interval is the range in which we can expect the true value of the dependent variable to lie for a specified level of probability. The greater the s_e, the larger the confidence interval for the estimate of our dependent variable. At the 95 per cent confidence level, the interval is $\hat{y} \pm 2.306s_e$. As the number of observations increases to, say 30 or more, this interval may be readily approximated as $\hat{y} \pm 2s_e$.

4 It is frequently argued that R^2, as defined above, yields a slightly optimistic indication of the goodness of fit of the regression line to the population data from which the sample is drawn. An adjusted R^2 is sometimes accordingly calculated. It is defined as $R^2_{adj} = R^2 - m(1 - R^2)/(n - m - 1)$ where n = the number of observations and m = the number of independent variables. See, for example, Norusis, *The SPSS Guide to Data Analysis for SPSS^x* (Chicago: SPSS 1986), 140.

5 Although we used the t distribution to test the hypothesis that $b = 0$, it can readily be seen that the distribution may be used to test any hypothesized value of b.

Selected Readings

Chapter 1: Introduction

Isserman, A. 1984. "Projection, Forecast, and Plan: On the Future of Population Forecasting." *American Planning Association Journal* 50:208-21

Keyfitz, N. 1982. "Can Knowledge Improve Forecasts?" *Population and Development Review* 8:730-51

Pittenger, D.B. 1977. "Population Forecasting Standards: Some Considerations Concerning Their Necessity and Content." *Demography* 14:363-68

Wachs, M. 1982. "Ethical Dilemmas in Forecasting for Public Policy." *Public Administration Review* 42:562-67

Chapter 2: Mathematical Extrapolation I

Bossard, E.G. 1992. "Curve Fitting/Extrapolation." In *Spreadsheet Models for Urban and Regional Analysis*, ed. R.G. Klosterman, R.K. Brail, and E.G. Bossard. New Brunswick, NJ: Center for Urban Policy Research, Rutgers University, 45-68

Croxton, F.E., D.J. Cowden, and S. Klein. 1967. "Analysis of Time Series: Secular Trends II – Non-Linear Trends." In *Applied General Statistics*. Englewood Cliffs, NJ: Prentice-Hall, 389-418

Dickey, J.W., and T.M. Watts. 1978. "Regression between Two Variables." In *Analytical Techniques in Urban and Regional Planning*. New York: McGraw-Hill, 124-44

Isserman, A.M. 1977. "The Accuracy of Population Projections for Sub-county Areas." *Journal of the American Institute of Planners* 43:247-59

Krueckeberg, D.A., and A.L. Silvers. 1974. "Projecting Populations." In *Urban Planning Analysis: Methods and Models*. New York: John Wiley and Sons, 259-87

Chapter 3: Mathematical Extrapolation II

Cervero, R. 1987. "Forecasting on the PC." *American Planning Association Journal* 53:510-20

Croxton, F.E., D.J. Cowden, and S. Klein. 1967. "Analysis of Time Series: Secular Trends II – Non-Linear Trends." In *Applied General Statistics*. Englewood Cliffs, NJ: Prentice-Hall, 250-84

Farnum, N.R., and L.W. Stanton. 1989. "Measuring Forecast Accuracy." In *Quantitative Forecasting Methods*. Boston: PWS-Kent, 22-31

Gabbour I. 1993. "SPOP: Small-Area Population Projection." In *Spreadsheet Models for Urban and Regional Analysis*, ed. R.G. Klosterman, R.K. Brail, and E.G. Bossard. New Brunswick, NJ: Centre for Urban Policy Research, Rutgers University, 69-84

Krueckeberg, D.A., and A.L. Silvers. 1974. "Projecting Populations." In *Urban Planning Analysis: Methods and Models*. New York: John Wiley and Sons, 259-87

Statistics Canada. 1981. *How Communities Can Use Statistics*. Ottawa: Supply and Services

Chapter 4: Comparative Methods

Isserman, A.M. 1977. "The Accuracy of Population Projections for Sub-County Areas." *Journal of the American Institute of Planners* 43:247-59

Isard, W. 1960. "Ratio Methods." In *Methods of Regional Analysis*. Cambridge, MA: MIT Press, 15-18

Krueckeberg, D.A., and A.L. Silvers. 1974. "The Comparative Method" and "Forecasts with Ratios." In *Urban Planning Analysis: Methods and Models*. New York: Wiley and Sons, 266-70

Oppenheim, N. 1980. "The Comparative Methods." In *Applied Models in Urban and Regional Analysis*. Englewood Cliffs, NJ: Prentice-Hall, 42-4

Smith, S.K. 1984. *Population Projections: What Do We Really Know?* Gainesville: Bureau of Economic and Business Research, University of Florida

Chapter 5: Cohort-Survival Population Model

Heer, D.M. 1975. *Society and Population*. Englewood Cliffs, NJ: Prentice-Hall

Olshansky, S.J. 1988. "On Forecasting Mortality." *The Milbank Quarterly* 66:482-530

Seward, S.B. 1987. *Demographic Change and the Canadian Economy: An Overview*. Ottawa: Institute for Research on Public Policy

Statistics Canada. 1984a. *Current Demographic Analysis: Fertility in Canada*. Cat. no. 91-524E, occasional. Ottawa: Supply and Services

–. 1984b. *Fertility in Canada: From Baby-Boom to Baby-Bust*. Cat. no. 91-524E, occasional. Ottawa: Supply and Services

–. 1987. *Report on the Demographic Situation in Canada 1986*. Cat no. 91-209E, annual. Ottawa: Supply and Services

Vlassoff, C. 1987. *Fertility and the Labour Force in Canada Critical Issues*. Ottawa: International Development Research Institute

Willekens, F.J. 1990. "Demographic Forecasting: State-of-the-Art and Research Needs." In *Emerging Issues in Demographic Research*, ed. C.A. Hazeu and G.A.B. Frinking. New York: Elsevier, 9-66

Chapter 6: Migration Models

Cadwallader, M. 1992. *Migration and Residential Mobility: Macro and Micro Approaches*. Madison: University of Wisconsin Press

Clark, W.A.V. 1986. *Human Migration*. Beverly Hills, CA: Sage

Isserman, A. 1986. "Forecasting Birth and Migration Rates: The Theoretical Foundation." In *Population Change and the Economy: Social Science Theories and Models*, ed. A. Isserman. Boston: Kluwer-Nijhoff, 3-30

Molho, I. 1986. "Theories of Migration: A Review." *Scottish Journal of Political Economy* 33:396-419

Nam, C.B., W.J. Serow, and D.F. Sly. 1990. *International Handbook on Internal Migration*. New York: Greenwood Press

Serow, W.J., C.B. Nam, D.F. Sly, and R.H. Weller, eds. 1990. *Handbook on International Migration*. New York: Greenwood Press

Simmons, J. 1981. "Population Forecasting: How Little We Know," *Plan Canada* 21 (3):75-84

Willekens, F.J. 1990. "Demographic Forecasting: State of the Art and Research Needs." In *Emerging Issues in Demographic Research*, ed. C.A. Hazeu and G.A.B. Frinking. New York: Elsevier, 9-66

Appendix A: Linear Regression

Achen, C.H. 1982. *Interpreting and Using Regression*. Beverly Hills: Sage

Lewis-Beck, M.S. 1989. *Applied Regression*. Beverly Hills: Sage

Norusis, M.J. 1986. *The SPSS Guide to Data Analysis for SPSS^r*. Chicago: SPSS

Appendix B: Logarithms

Burington, R.S. 1948. *Handbook of Mathematical Tables and Formulas*. Sandusky, OH: Handbook Publishers, 97-101

Hummelbrunner, S.A. 1982. *Contemporary Business Mathematics*. Scarborough, ON: Prentice-Hall, 205-9

Krueckeberg, D.A., and A.L. Silvers. 1974. *Urban Planning Analysis: Methods and Models*. New York: Wiley and Sons, 270-75

Index